Angola Beloved

A story of God's faithfulness

T. Ernest Wilson

GOSPEL FOLIO PRESS
www.gospelfolio.com

First edition printed by Loizeaux Brothers December 1967

Second edition published by
GOSPEL FOLIO PRESS
304 Killaly Street West
Port Colborne, ON, Canada L3K 6A6
1-800-952-2382
www.gospelfolio.com

Scripture taken from the King James Version, unless otherwise noted.
Copyright © 1982 by Thomas Nelson, Inc.
Used by permission. All rights reserved.

ISBN 978-1-897117-44-2

Cover design by Rachel Brooks

Inside Sketches by J. Boyd Nicholson

Printed in the United States of America.

Elizabeth
oct 2008
Conference

Angola
Beloved
A story of God's faithfulness

To that noble band of men and women who have devoted their lives to the spread of the gospel in Angola, our partners and fellow helpers, the messengers of the churches and the glory of Christ...

And to our African children in the faith, many of whom have been faithful unto death and some of whom are in prison for Christ's sake...

This book is affectionately dedicated.

Mr. and Mrs. Wilson in Angola

Contents

Foreword

In the fall of 1923, the world was gradually coming together after the horror and destruction of World War I but there was still great instability in many parts of Europe. The governments of Bulgaria and Spain were both overthrown in military coups. Vladimir Lenin suffered a third stroke and stepped down from the Soviet government. A young thirty-four year old Adolf Hitler led an unsuccessful revolt against the German government and in the United States, President Harding died in office and was replaced by Calvin Coolidge.

But in Belfast, Northern Ireland, there was only one thing on the mind of twenty-one year old T. Ernest Wilson and that was the millions of lost souls in Africa who had never heard the gospel. When only eighteen years old, he had listened to missionaries tell of the great spiritual need in Angola and made a commitment in his heart to serve the Lord among those people. That heart-felt commitment became a reality when he was commended to the work of the Lord in Africa several years later by a small working-class assembly in Belfast. He not only had a desire to be obedient but had also been deeply impressed by the faith and testimony of men like George Mueller, who had put their confidence entirely in the Lord, never asking for money. Believing this to be the way God intended us to live, he made it a practice to never mention his material needs to anyone but the Lord.

In the book, God is Faithful, compiled by Jabe Nicholson, a story is told that perfectly illustrates what living a life of faith really means. As T. Ernest Wilson was standing on the Belfast docks preparing to leave for Africa, a kind brother pressed two gold coins into his hand, saying, "If you are ever down to your last penny, there is something to fall back on." As a testament to God's faithfulness and provision, T. Ernest Wilson still had those two gold coins over seventy years later. God had fully met their needs during a life of service to Him.

This book is an account both of hardship and joy, as well as setbacks and accomplishments. It is a riveting story of danger, adventure and opportunity for the Lord. But more than all that, it is a practical example of how we as believers should be living. We do pray that this updated edition will reach a new generation of believers, both young and old who desire to serve the Lord faithfully, putting into practice the words of Philippians 4:19, *"But my God shall supply all your need according to His riches in glory by Christ Jesus."*

Introduction

Africa the sleeping giant is awake! He is flexing his muscles and having serious growing pains. What is he thinking and where is he headed? Politically he is having trouble settling down. Geographically the country is shaped like a huge question mark. The whole world in the meantime is holding its breath and reserving its judgment.

One of the earliest parts of Africa to become known to the Europeans is Angola. The Portuguese have been there for four hundred and eighty years, and yet perhaps it is the least known to the civilized world. For centuries it has been an African backwater. When it is mentioned in polite society, some still innocently ask: "Oh, is that where the Angora cats come from?"

Our main interest in this book will not be with politics or geography, important as these are today, but with a work of God which has been going on in the hearts and lives of its native people.

It should be kept in mind that Roman Catholic missions and missionaries have been in Angola since the earliest days of Portuguese occupation. Many of the priests today are foreigners, yet Roman Catholicism is the state-recognized and subsidized religion.

The first Protestant missionary to reach Angola was David Livingstone, who in his historic journey across Africa from east to west in 1854 passed through Angola. Then came the Baptist

11

Missionary Society in 1878, followed by the American Board of Commissioners for Foreign Missions in 1880, and the United Church of Canada in 1886. The Board of Foreign Missions of the Methodist Episcopal Church (U.S.A.) commenced work in the Luanda area in 1884. Later on came the Mission Philafricaine from Switzerland (1897), and the South African General Mission (International) in 1914. The Seventh Day Adventists have been in the country since 1924. Since 1924 no other Protestant missionary group has been granted permission to open new work in Angola.

The pioneer of the work described in this book was Frederick Stanley Arnot from Scotland, who first came to Angola in 1886. He was in church fellowship with groups of Christians popularly known as "Plymouth Brethren" or "Open Brethren." Arnot was the typical pioneer, surveying and opening up new areas and inspiring others to take up the task of laying foundations and building up the work.

Missionaries from the Brethren are commended to the mission field individually by their home assemblies, each assembly being autonomous. There are, however, a number of service organizations in various countries, which provide channels for forwarding gifts and funds, and also circulate information and news from mission fields to those at home.

"Christian Missions in Many Lands," made up of representatives from a number of these service organizations, is the liaison between assembly missionaries and the governments concerned.

After Arnot came Charles Albert Swan from Sunderland, England. He spent twenty-five years in founding the missionary center at Chilonda in Bié, among the Umbundu-speaking people. Frederick T. Lane from London, England, pioneered the work in Capango, also in Bié. Thomas Louttit and William Maitland, a Scot and an Irishman from the United States, were the pioneers among the Chokwe people, arriving in 1904. Dr. Walter Fisher and Cyril Bird from England opened the work among the Luena-speaking people in 1890. This work has been carried on for many years by James MacPhie from Scotland, by Albert Horton from the United States, and by Nigel Arnot, son of the original pioneer.

As well as these men, who laid the foundations, there has been a succession of honored and faithful men and women who have been responsible for developing and consolidating the work and who continue to the present day, also commended by and in church fellowship with assemblies of Brethren.

The object of all assembly missionary work is the planting of New Testament churches on native soil, completely autonomous, with no foreign domination or control, dependent on the Holy Spirit alone for guidance and progress. While medical, educational, and social work is vigorously carried on, the supreme object is the establishment of the indigenous church.

Few parts of Africa have been so thoroughly evangelized with the gospel of Jesus Christ as has Angola. Most parts of the country have been penetrated by pioneer missionaries, both black and white.

In many a forest clearing and around practically all the towns are to be found companies of African Christians, meeting in a simple primitive way, completely indigenous, seeking to spread the gospel among their own people. Their only literature is a Bible or New Testament translated into their own language, a hymnbook which they love—for they are a musical, singing people, and maybe one or two pamphlets on baptism and church order. They labor with their hands for daily food and supplies and they preach for the love of it, not for pay. The buildings in which they meet are mostly mud-and-wattle shacks with grass roofs and dirt floors. The only pieces of furniture are a rickety table, some log benches, a hurricane lamp, and an easel and blackboard. Outside, suspended from the branch of a tree is an old brake drum or a piece of iron railroad line, which serves as a bell to call the people, as most of them do not possess a watch or clock.

There are literally hundreds of such groups in Angola today and they are increasing all the time in spite of much difficulty from various sources. Some of the more prosperous have a brick building with a tile roof and glass windows. These have been financed and built by the Africans themselves. This work is not an organization needing support from over-seas, but is a living organism. It has vitality and will grow. It may be crushed in one place but will spring up in another.

Two factors have largely contributed to the phenomenal success of missionary work along these lines in Angola. First is the character and the vision of the men who founded it. They put good material into the foundations. Second is the comparatively good material with which the missionaries have had to work. The Ovimbundu and Chokwe tribes especially have well repaid the many years of training and discipline expended on them. Some tribes have a background of slavery and abysmally low moral standards and are consequently disappointing in their response to the work bestowed on them. But Angola has been fortunate in the sturdy and intelligent types which have produced such excellent results.

The writer has had personal contact with this work for nearly forty years and has watched it grow from small beginnings to its present proportions. This book is an attempt to describe how that development took place. Here is a simple and factual account of some of the difficulties and heartaches as well as the joys and blessings involved in laboring in a pioneer field.

PART I

Africa's Mystic Spell

Africa has always been a land of mystery; its very shape suggests a huge question mark. For centuries it was called "The Dark Continent." Its geography and the sources of its river systems were matters for speculation. Early maps had a chain of mountains running across its center, named, for want of a better term, "The Mountains of the Moon." The first Europeans who penetrated some distance into the interior brought back exaggerated and horrendous tales of the land and its barbarous inhabitants. But the country has always had a mysterious drawing power and fascination for those who have spent any time within its borders. There is a nostalgic pull to come back.

Africa is a country of cruelty. Consider the centuries of the slave trade when millions of human beings were sold like cattle or sheep; when little children who could not survive the long journey to the coast were knocked on the head against a tree; when cannibalism was common practice and ritual murder was the order of the day.

It is a country of fear: fear of the unknown, fear of evil spirits, fear of death, fear of wild animals and insects, and above all, fear of ruthless men who have no compassion or conscience.

It is also a country of darkness. At night when the sun goes in, the darkness takes over. Twilight lasts but a few minutes and then night, black and sinister, comes down. The black man barricades himself in his hut and nature, red in tooth and claw, goes on the prowl. No human being travels alone at night if he can help it.

But Africa is not all wild animals and snakes and plagues. It is the most fascinating country in the world. It is a land of sounds: the cricket in the evening; the cry of a baby goat or a baby African, which are almost identical; insects rustling, frogs croaking; monotonous drumming in the night; the cry of the *mutambi* calling the spirits when someone is near death; the songbirds at dawn; and the wailing madman with wooden shackles on his hands and feet, tethered to a log.

Africa is also a land of smells: burnt grass in the dry sea-son; the warm earth after the first rains; parched corn roasted on the open fire; pungent tobacco smoke in the villages; ripe meat left too long; and unwashed bodies close together in a meeting. But the sounds and smells give one an indescribable homesick long-ing and remind one of the lines written to "Mother Africa."

> There are millions who know nothing of your spell,
> And revile you for your cruelty and pain.
> Out in Africa they say, men are lost and thrown away.
> We know better, Mother Africa, your children come
> to stay, And they never climb a city wall again.

Most people who have spent a good part of their life in Af-rica, and who for some reason have had to leave, have an irre-sistible longing to go back. I know people whose homes were looted, who saw their friends tortured and killed, and who themselves had to flee for their lives, who, when things settled down, were counting the days until they could return.

William Maitland, one of the pioneers of missionary work in Chokweland in Angola, was invalided home to Chicago after spending nearly fifty years in Africa. He was eighty years of age. In his early days in Africa he nearly died of starvation dur-ing a famine, on several occasions had been unconscious with malaria with no one to care for him but a native boy, and had been bitten by ticks and bedbugs and tsetse flies. He was liv-ing in comparative comfort in America, honored and loved by a wide circle of friends. He pleaded with me, with tears in his eyes, "Please ask these hardhearted people to allow me to go back to Africa." What makes a man feel that way? It is the mystic spell of the land.

This is the land I have learned to love and which I regard as home. Some of my best friends on earth, both black and white, are there. There are many children in the faith, some of whom have literally risked their lives for us. Even today, exiled by circumstances, there is a heavy pull at the heart-strings to be back among them again. Perhaps some day!

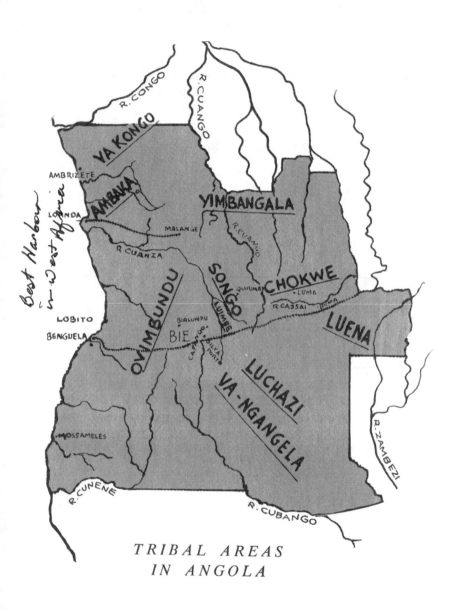

TRIBAL AREAS
IN ANGOLA

Angola—The Country

Africa in 1966 had thirty-seven independent nations. But Angola in West Africa and Mozambique in East Africa are not among their number. They are still Portuguese possessions, controlled and governed from Lisbon in Portugal. The Portuguese do not call them colonies, but overseas provinces of Portugal. Diogo Cão, a Portuguese mariner, discovered the mouth of the Congo in 1482, placed a stone cross on a headland, thus claiming the country for Portugal.

Being in Angola for four hundred and eighty years, the Portuguese naturally regard it as theirs! They have no plans or intention of handing over control to an African government. On the contrary, the Africans are regarded as Portuguese citizens and, if they fulfill certain standards of civilization, are allowed to vote. For instance, they are expected to wear European clothes, eat their food at a table with their family, pay the Portuguese military tax instead of the native head tax, and especially be able to read and write and speak the Portuguese language. A comparatively small number of Africans, perhaps five per cent, fulfill these conditions.

For this reason the Africans are encouraged to learn and speak the Portuguese language and become integrated into Portuguese society. All educational work is oriented with this object in mind. There has never been a color bar in Angola. Portuguese men frequently live with and sometimes marry Negro women. But there is definitely a social bar. The Portuguese are very caste conscious but color, per se, does not enter into it.

Economically Portugal cannot afford to lose its African possessions. Angola and Mozambique are immensely rich in natural resources, while Portugal is correspondingly poor. Money and raw materials flow in one direction from Africa to Lisbon. Without this Portugal would go bankrupt. Angolan independence would be disastrous for Portugal.

Angola has a land area of 484,800 square miles, twice the size of Texas and four times the size of the United Kingdom. It is bounded on the north by the Congo River and on the south by the Kunene. It has a coastline between these two rivers of 1,015 miles. Its eastern border is the Congo Republic in the north and Zambia in the south.

Angola is divided by the twelfth parallel into two distinct climatic zones. The northern is hot, tropical, and moist, with a small rainfall on the coast. The interior is high and mountainous with heavy torrential rains during the wet season from October till April. The southern zone is temperate, being influenced by the cold Benguela current, which sweeps in from the Atlantic and washes that part of the coast. From the coast the ground rises sharply, soon attaining an altitude of 5,500 feet, forming the fertile and comparatively healthy Bié plateau.

No part of Central Africa could be accurately described as a health resort and on these highlands malaria is common and blackwater fever is not unknown. But with ordinary precautions, two-thirds of the area of the interior of Angola is suitable for European occupation, especially the districts of Benguela, Bié, Moxico (pronounced Moshiko), and parts of Malange.

There are two seasons in the year, the wet and the dry. As already intimated, the wet season lasts from October till April and the dry season from May till September. During the months of June and July, especially in the highlands, the nights are cold, ice forming occasionally on the river valleys. Towards the end of the dry season, the plains are swept with bush fires which burn up the rank grass, leaving the living trees and bushes. This is the annual spring cleaning, when hordes of vermin are destroyed and the whole country purified.

It would be hard to imagine a more beautiful sight than that after the first rain falls. The whole country parched with the burning sun springs to life, and the plains are carpeted with various colored flowers and undergrowth. Rivers and streams which flow all the year round are found everywhere on the plateau. On the whole, Angola could be considered one of the most pleasant parts of Central Africa.

Luanda, the capital of Angola is one of the oldest occupied cities in West Africa. It has a population of 160,000, of whom about 45,000 are white. It has been largely rebuilt during the past thirty years. Many of the buildings are colored with pastel shades which give it a pleasant and even beautiful appearance from the sea. But many of the old buildings still remain, which provide a link with the bad old days of the slave trade. It is the seat of government and has the residence of the governor general, who is appointed from Lisbon.

The port of Lobito has the best harbor in West Africa. In 1900 this mushroom town consisted of nothing more than a few fishermen's huts on a spit of sand, on which the sun beat mercilessly. A few miles away along the shore lay the old Portuguese town of Benguela, the terminus in past days of the slave, ivory, and rubber trade from the interior. Slaves were still being taken to the coast for sale as late as 1908 but about 1910 the traffic had come to an end.

The development of Lobito lies to the credit of one far-seeing and hardheaded Scotsman, Robert Williams. Williams as a young man was a close associate and loyal disciple of the late Cecil Rhodes, after whom Rhodesia was named. Williams was Rhodes' righthand man in the tremendous enterprise of bringing to pass the latter's dream of building a railway from the Cape to Cairo. While surveying the route, Williams heard about the copper deposits of Katanga. Experience had taught him that the great mineral beds always lay in the watersheds and he deduced that the area between the headwaters of the Congo and the Zambesi would repay exploration.

It must not be forgotten, however, that copper was known

to exist in this region and had been worked by the natives from time immemorial. They used copper crosses for currency. The early missionaries too had been in Katanga and knew about the copper deposits, years before Williams got there.

In 1900 Williams organized a company to explore and export the copper. But how was the copper to reach the sea and the markets of Europe and America? An intensive study of the map and the idea of a railway from Katanga to Benguela in Angola was born in Williams' brain. But Benguela had no harbor. Ships dropped anchor offshore and landed their passengers and cargo in lighters. A harbor must be found. The indomitable Scot found a spot less than 20 miles from Benguela where a spit of sand ran parallel with the shore, enclosing a deep water lagoon and forming a magnificent natural port. The railway line was started in 1903, the frontier of the Congo was reached in 1928, and the final link with Elizabethville in Katanga completed in 1931.

When it is realized that the distance from Katanga to Capetown is 2,470 miles and that the railway to Lobito in Angola shortened the land journey to the sea by 1,200 miles and that Lobito is 1,450 miles nearer Europe, it will be readily seen that the future of the port is assured. It is the natural outlet for the mineral wealth and the produce of Central Africa.

The diamond mines at Dundo, in the far northeastern corner of the country, is another valuable source of revenue to Angola. The inner Casai, a thousand miles north of Kimberley, was once a black man's kingdom, which for a white man to enter meant a sudden and terrible death. Even the great Livingstone was warned off and kept clear.

Diamonds were first found by men who, to save their camp from flooding in the rainy season, dug a trench to drain off the water, and found diamonds sparkling in the gravel. The black man's empire was doomed. Portuguese troops very soon put an end to any resistance. A syndicate with wide ramifications was formed. It was named "Diamang" and backed by international financiers. A modern town sprang up in the jungle with electric light, concrete houses, and all the gadgets of civilization.

The grand thing about the place is its isolation. Dundo is a strictly private preserve from which the outsider is rigidly excluded and a permit to enter is exceedingly difficult to obtain. Huge trucks with ten-ton loads plow through the wilderness from Luso on the Benguela railway, six hundred twenty-five miles to Dundo with machinery and provisions, and on the return trip bring out diamonds. Inside half-naked Negroes splash about and shovel in the mud for the fabulous wealth. These laborers are recruited by a system of forced contract labor and come from many far distant parts of the country. Each worker must dig out and turn over a certain quota of earth every day. The Portuguese government is given a certain percentage of free shares in the enterprise, as well as receiving revenue from the output. Practically all the technicians of foreign nationality, who worked for the company at its inception, have been eliminated and replaced by Portuguese. Dundo is not clearly marked on many maps, but it is in the Lunda district. The remarkable way in which the door was opened for the spread of the gospel in the diamond fields is a fascinating story in itself and will be told in a later chapter.

Angola—The People

Angola today has a multiracial society, the majority of the population being of Negro Bantu stock, with a minority of white Portuguese and *mulattoes* of every shade, the result of centuries of the white man intermarrying with the black. Its first inhabitants, as far as we can discover, were bushmen and Pygmies. Small remnants of these primitive people still remain around the Kalahari Desert in the south. They were expert hunters, shooting poisoned arrows, meat being their principal food. When they couldn't find game, they existed on roots and insects.

Then about A.D. 1000 the Hottentots invaded Central Africa. They brought with them the beginnings of civilization, cultivating the ground and making tools of copper and iron.

But another migration was already going on. Tradition says that about 2,000 years ago, the Bantu (an African word, meaning "people") started to move from their original home in the far north, where they were in contact with Egyptian and Persian influences.

The Bantus founded colonies all over Central Africa, conquering and practically exterminating the original inhabitants of the country. By the fourteenth to the sixteenth centuries they had invaded Angola. Soon the great Bantu race covered all of Central and South Africa.

But then, losing all contact with the outside world, and

being cut off from the ancient civilizations in the north, the Bantus settled down to a lazy existence. Life in the tropics was easy; fertile soil, abundant fish in the rivers and lakes, enormous herds of game on the rolling plains, all made for a life of leisure and contributed to their decadence. The Bantu race, which now numbers about fifty million, with perhaps three hundred languages and dialects, became an easy prey for any native adventurer who could gather a following of plunderers and carve out a kingdom for himself. These were the people that the Portuguese found in Angola when their mariners and explorers landed at the end of the fifteenth century.

Today there are three great tribal divisions in Angola, divided into about fifty language groups:

The Ambakista tribes consist of the remnants of the old Congo kingdom, having its headquarters at San Salvador near the mouth of the Congo and stretching as far south as Luanda and Novo Redondo. The interior tribes call them the *A-Mbaka* ("coast people").

The fisher tribes' ancestral home was the upper reaches of the Zambesi, from which they spread along the courses of the great rivers. The Luchazi, Luimbe, and Songos belong to this group. They speak different dialects but are closely interrelated.

The hunting tribes live mostly in the forest, eking out a living by cultivation, barter, or collecting beeswax. The Lunda, Lovale, and Chokwe all come from a common stock and had their origin in the Lu-unda country on the east side of the Lulwa River, in what is now the Republic of Congo. The capital village of Mwata-Yamvo, the paramount chief, is there to the present day. It is interesting to note, in passing, that this is the area from which Moise Tshombe, the first premier of Congo, came.

The Ovimbundu tribe, speaking the Umbundu language, with its headquarters in Bié (Silva Porto) and Bailundu (Vila Teixeira da Silva) in Angola, is widely spread across Central Africa. They are an intelligent, hard-working, and shrewd people. During the old slave raiding days, and when the ivory and rubber trade was at its height, trading caravans of Ovimbundu penetrated as far as Tanganyika, now Tanzania. Interior people call them the Yimbali. Their ancestral chief, Viye, married a Songo maiden named Cahanda and built their capital village near to where the city of Silva Porto now stands. The Portuguese name, Bié, which is given to the whole district, is a corruption of the name of the chief, Viye.

The Chokwes are a proud, independent, outspoken race who despised the Ovimbundu as the slaves of the white man. They were the old highway robbers of Central Africa, plundering the trade caravans as they went to and from the coast. All the young men had the prefix "Mwa" attached to their name. It means a prince of royal blood. But then all Chokwe blood was royal blood! They cut their teeth into a V-shape, carried a knife in their belt, and swaggered as if they were the lords of creation. In the early days they refused to dirty their hands with manual labor. Missionary work among them for many years was difficult, but steady faithful plodding has paid handsome spiritual dividends in indigenous churches, not only in Angola, but much farther afield.

The Portuguese, of course, are the ruling class of the country. Emigration from Portugal is encouraged in every way and, especially in the past thirty years, they have been coming in ever-increasing numbers. The object is to Latinize the country and make it an overseas province of Portugal in reality as well as in name.

To encourage white Portuguese emigration the Angolan government has set up several agricultural experimental areas. The government offers to any Portuguese farmer, who is over 30 years old and married, a twenty-hectare (nearly fifty-acre) plot, with a cow, sheep, a brood sow, six chickens, six ducks, and some rabbits. But these efforts have had only a very limited success.

The black population of Angola is around four million. The white population remained constant or perhaps even declined in the uncertain decade from 1930 to 1940, but in the following ten years the white residents rose from 44,000 to 78,000 and to 110,000 by 1955.

According to recent statistics, in 1962 the over-all population of Angola was 4,855,219, the whites numbering 172,529 and the *mulattoes* 60,000. Thus it can be seen that black outnumbered white about 20 to 1. The New York Times for January 27, 1967 shows the population figure as 5,154,000.

David Livingstone

Pioneers

The names of Dr. David Livingstone and of Frederick Stanley Arnot will always be associated with the opening up of Central Africa. Livingstone was born of humble parents in Blantyre, Scotland, in 1813. He studied in Glasgow and received his medical diploma in November 1840. He first had thought of going to China as a medical missionary but his way was blocked by the Opium War which was going on at the time. Dr. Robert Moffat of South Africa was home on furlough in 1840 and, after meeting him in London, England, and as a result of a long earnest conversation, Livingstone decided to go to Africa instead. He landed in South Africa in 1841, settled at a place called Kuruman, and married Moffat's daughter, Mary, in 1844. He had gone to Africa under the auspices of the London Missionary Society, but constantly chafed at their orders that he stay in one place and carry on a settled work.

The interior of Africa at that time was practically unknown to the outside world. Across the maps of Central Africa was written, "The Mountains of the Moon," and little else. No one knew where the sources of the Nile, the Zambesi, or the Congo were located. Livingstone's great task was to open up the "Dark Continent" to the rest of the world. He wrote to the directors of the London Missionary Society that he was at their disposal "to go anywhere—provided it be forward." Later he wrote to his father-in-law, "I shall open up a path into the interior or perish."

Finally he sent his wife and children to England and started into his lifework of exploring the unknown regions of Central Africa. With a few African natives carrying his scanty belongings, he covered thousands of miles on foot. Often seriously ill with malaria, in danger of his life from wild beasts and wilder men, he faithfully pursued his idea, but at the cost of his life. He discovered Lake Ngami (1849), the upper Zambesi (1851), Victoria Falls (1856), Lake Nyassa (1859), Lake Moero (1867), and Lake Bangweolo (1868). On his last journey he was exploring the sources of the Nile when he died alone in a grass hut in what is now known as Zambia. The date was May 1, 1873. The end is described by Blaikie in his book, *The Personal Life of David Livingstone*:

> At last they [his African carriers] got him to Chitambo's village in Ilala, where they had put him under the eaves of a house during the drizzling rain until the hut they were building should be got ready. Then they laid him on a rough bed in the hut, where he spent the night. Next day he lay undisturbed...Nothing occurred to attract notice during the early part of the night, but at four in the morning, the boy who lay at his door, called in alarm for Susi, fearing that their master was dead. By the candle still burning they saw him, not in bed, but kneeling at the bedside, with his head buried in his hands upon the pillow: he had passed away on the furthest of all his journeys, and without a single attendant. But he had died in the act of prayer...commending Africa—his own dear Africa, with all her woes and sins and wrongs—to the Avenger of the oppressed and the Redeemer of the lost.

Livingstone's African attendants then made arrangements for drying and embalming the body. They removed and buried the heart and the viscera under a tree. For fourteen days the body was dried in the sun. After being wrapped in calico and the legs bent inwards at the knees, it was enclosed in a large piece of bark in the form of a cylinder. Over this a piece of sailcloth was sewed; and the package was lashed to a pole, so as to be carried by two men. They then set out on the long march to the coast. Their destination was Zanzibar. The remains were there placed on a ship and taken to England. On Saturday, April 18, 1874, the body of the great missionary pioneer was committed to its last resting place near the center of the nave in Westminster Abbey. Among the pall-bearers were H. M. Stanley, who "found" Livingstone in Africa when he had been lost for two years, and one of the faithful African carriers who had taken his body to the coast.

The following lines appeared in *Punch*, an English magazine, at the time of the funeral:

> Open the Abbey gates and let him in
> To sleep with King and Statesman, Chief and Sage.
> The Missionary came of weaver kin
> Yet great by work that brooks no lower wage.
> He needs no epitaph to guard a name
> That men shall prize while worthy work is done.
> He lived and died for God, be this his fame;
> Let marble crumble, this is Livingstone.

Livingstone was the first evangelical missionary to reach Angola. In his epoch-making journey from Linyanti on the Zambesi to Luanda in 1853 he crossed the country from east to west on foot and then, on his return, from west to east. While his name is linked with geographical exploration, his primary object was to reach the people with the gospel and this he faithfully carried out.

Frederick Stanley Arnot was born September 12, 1858 in Glasgow, Scotland. As a boy he became interested in going to Africa through seeing the relics of the great pioneer, sent home after Livingstone's death. He was inspired by Living-stone's example and determined to give his life to carry on the task Livingstone had begun. He was of the same blood, breed, and belief. With the support and prayers of groups of interested Christians in Great Britain, he left for Africa when he was twenty-one years of age. He had no mission board at his back but went out simply trusting God to supply his need. He reached Natal in Southeast Africa in 1881. The same year he pressed on north to Barotseland, now a part of Zambia, where he spent eighteen months.

Arnot was a shy, unassuming, and utterly dedicated man. Sir Ralph Williams, in his book, *How I Became Governor*, has this to say about Arnot after meeting him at Victoria Falls in 1884:

> Mr. Arnot, the missionary, was a remarkable man. I had many talks with him. He was the simplest and most earnest of men. He lived a life of great hardship under the care of the king of the Barotse, and taught his children. I remember his telling me with some pride that his pupils had mastered the alphabet. I have seen many missionaries under varied circumstances, but such an absolutely forlorn man, existing on from day to day, almost hopeless, without any appliances which make life bearable, I have never seen. He was imbued with one desire, and that was to do God service. Whether it could be best done that way I will not here question, but he looked neither to right or left, caring nothing for himself if he could get one to believe; at least so he struck me. And I have honored him ever since as being as near his Master as anyone I ever saw.

In Barotseland Arnot had met Silva Porto, a Portuguese trader, who invited him to accompany him on the long journey west to Portuguese Angola and provided him with a riding ox for the journey. From Porto's home at Belmonte, on the Bié highlands in Angola, he went on to Catumbela at the coast, thus completing the crossing of Africa from east to west. Much of this journey was done on foot involving incredible hardships. At Catumbela he replenished his food boxes, and purchased a scanty supply of trade goods. Then he retraced his steps to Silva Porto's home, about 350 miles from the coast.

In all his journeys across Africa, Arnot had heard the name of Mushidi, an African king who ruled over a wide area, in those days called Garenganze, but now called Katanga, the southern province of the Congo. Mushidi had carved out a kingdom for himself by butchery and pillage. His fame spread far and wide. He was known to the Portuguese in the far west, who had provided him with a *mulatto* wife, but at the same time he was reputed to have more than five hundred concubines. The Arabs from the east were frequent visitors at his capital, engaged in the slave trade. Roving bands of native traders, seeking for barter in ivory, rubber, and slaves, penetrated his country from the west. Constant intertribal warfare had created ideal conditions for the vile traffic in human beings.

Long slave caravans were to be met with on the journey to the coast, dying men and women and little children cast into the bush, their hands hacked off, to facilitate the removal of their shackles, were a common sight. In comparatively recent times it was not unusual to see the whitened bones of dead slaves lying beside the path on the long journey to the coast, and the shackles dangling from the branches of the roadside bushes. The shackle was simply a block of heavy wood with a slot cut in the middle, just large enough for the hands or feet to be slipped through, and a wooden peg driven between them, so that they could not be withdrawn. These were worn at night and carried by the slave during the day on top of his load. It was reckoned that only one out of five slaves, captured in the interior, reached the coast alive. If a woman who had a small child happened to die, the child was killed by dashing its head against a tree.

Arnot decided to visit Mushidi's country and take the gospel of Christ to this hotbed of sin and bloodshed. He parted with Silva Porto with regret. The Portuguese trader had shown him much kindness and had urged him to remain permanently in Angola and start his mission work there. But Arnot felt he must see Mushidi first, and on October 13, 1885 he set out once more for the interior.

It was a long and perilous journey occupying several months, during which he endured much hardship and frustration. The African chiefs were then in complete control. The road into the interior had literally to be bought by presents of cloth to every little petty potentate who blocked the road. Speaking of this journey Arnot wrote: "I had three Garenganze men as my guides. They were sent out from time to time by their chief to look for traders, and seemed to think that they had caught a fish in me, and evidently thought their mission fulfilled. Well, be it so. The Garenganze chief knows of nothing better to search for than traders, but the living God may be pleased to send him His precious Word."

Arnot finally reached Mushidi's kingdom early in 1886. His arrival in Katanga brought him face to face with barbaric splendor as seen in Mushidi's court. "Off with his head" was not fiction, like the words of Lewis Carroll's queen in *Alice in Wonderland*, but a daily fact in the African chief's village. His stockaded kraal was decorated pole by pole with the skulls of his hapless victims. Outside his house were tables piled high with the heads of those whom his executioners had decapitated. Just five years after Arnot had landed in Africa, he entered Mushidi's amazing capital, and there, a few miles along the ridge of one of the hills, he built the first little mission house in that pagan land.

Arnot continued for eighteen months alone at Mushidi's capital and then to his great joy on December 16, 1887 he was joined by Charles A. Swan of Sunderland, England, and by William Faulkner of Hamilton, Ontario, Canada. These two, from different parts of the world, had heard of Arnot's work, and decided to come to his help. Both were connected with similar New Testament churches as had sent out Arnot.

When Swan arrived at Benguela on the West African coast, he was accompanied by Peter Scott from England, who had joined him in Lisbon. Hard walking for fourteen days brought them to Bailundu and then another seven days to Bié. Here it was evident that Scott's health could not stand the strain, so he decided to go back to England. Swan accompanied him back to the coast and then returned alone to the interior with the object of reaching Arnot. The weary journey to the point where Scott turned back was nearly accomplished for the third time, when a special runner overtook him, bringing the news that one named Faulkner, a Canadian, had arrived at the coast and wished to accompany him. There was no alternative but to retrace once more his steps to the coast and bring him in. Each of these five journeys was a distance of over 400 miles on foot on a 9-inch path through forests and plains, and sleeping on the ground at night in a tent or beside a fire.

The two men then started from Benguela at the coast late in September 1887 and after incredible difficulties and hard-ships arrived at Mushidi's capital in Katanga on December 16 of the same year. They had walked a distance of approximately 1,200 miles. When Arnot heard they were about to arrive, he put on his best clothes. With a crowd of savages looking on, the three men met under the shadow of the stockade surmounted by human skulls. They joined hands and sang, the words of the hymn beginning:

Jesus shall reign where'er the sun
Doth his successive journeys run;
His kingdom stretch from shore to shore
Till moons shall wax and wane no more.

At that time there was not a single African Christian in the country. All was pagan darkness. But these pioneers could look ahead in faith and see the mighty harvest that was to be reaped in Central Africa.

Arnot introduced the new arrivals to Mushidi. Swan describes his meeting with the chief as follows:

"On reaching the chief's enclosure we saw him coming out with a headdress of parrot's tail feathers, his body and arms covered with cloth of the most gaudy colors, and his face white with clay; and then came Kitompa, his head wife, riding in her litter and dressed in a similar manner to the chief. Then warriors came next walking very slowly and singing their doleful war song, while the skulls of their victims were to be seen, either in their hands or dangling at their waists. One even had a skull hanging from his teeth. They began their dance amidst the firing of guns and kept it up in a monotonous way. Then they retired in an orderly manner, and returned one by one, brandishing their spears, and laid their skulls at the feet of the chief. Then the head-man came forward and gave a long oration, after which he danced, and the women standing around carried him small presents. Kitompa made her speech, danced, received presents, and then retired. The chief then made his speech, and then made a lame attempt to dance. Mushidi's rule is most severe, yet we do not altogether condemn him in this, for in no other way could order be kept among his people, and it must be clearly understood that he only is chief, his authority is absolute."

Both Arnot and Swan were on terms of intimacy with Mushidi. Both were there before the Belgians came. While the chief condescendingly called them his slaves, yet it is evident that he both respected and trusted them. Being of British nationality, they could easily have influenced the king to hand over the protectorate of the country to the representatives of the British Queen Victoria. Some later blamed them because they didn't. Subsequent history could easily have been altered if they had. They little realized the issues that were at stake. But as missionaries and as servants of God, they took a strictly neutral stand and refused to allow their nationality to influence their conduct.

Three months after the arrival of Swan and Faulkner, in March 1888, Arnot left Katanga for the coast and England. Here he was warmly received. The Royal Geographic Society made him a Fellow and highly praised his explorations. His account of an open door and a waiting continent, told in a most unassuming manner, aroused deepest sympathy and widespread interest. When he returned to Africa in 1889 he was accompanied by a large party of recruits for the new mission field. This time his route was by the west coast. But disaster overtook them from the beginning. As the ship was dropping anchor in the harbor at Benguela in Angola, Robert J. Johnstone died of yellow fever. Then two of the party, Morris and Gall, died in one night of malaria at Bailundu, twelve days' march from the coast. Many weeks elapsed before the survivors reached their first halting place at Kuanjululu, 250 miles from the coast. Here Joseph Lynn was bitten by a mad dog and died from rabies.

From this point, three members of the party, Hugh Thompson from Armagh, Ireland, Fred Lane from London, England, and Dan Crawford from Greenock, Scotland, pressed on into Katanga. These three young missionaries arrived at Mushidi's capital on November 8, 1890, where they were warmly welcomed by Swan and Faulkner.

It was soon after the arrival of these reinforcements that the Belgians entered Katanga and built the first military fort on the Lofoi River fifty miles from Mushidi's stronghold. On December 19, 1891 the Belgians hoisted the Congo Free State flag, thus signifying that the country had been annexed by a European power.

The following day, after an unsatisfactory and most unfortunate conference between Mushidi and the Belgians, the chief was shot by a Belgian officer, who immediately paid the penalty, a score of flashing *assegais* thrust through this officer's quivering body. So ended the reign of the tyrant Mushidi.

After these events Fred Lane and Charles Swan returned to Angola and, along with Arnot, laid the foundations of missionary work in that Portuguese colony.

Arnot was the first white man to see the surpassing wealth of the Katanga mineral belt. He could have made a name and fame for himself as capitalist, financier, and captain of industry. Sir Robert Williams, who was largely responsible for developing the copper mines in Katanga and Zambia, and who worked in close collaboration with the late Cecil Rhodes, visited Angola in 1928. At an after-luncheon speech at Dondi, he stated that he owed his knowledge of the vast mineral resources of Katanga to Arnot, who could have made millions had he chosen to stake out mineral claims in that country. But Arnot deliberately turned his back on the gain of money in order to gain souls and to preach the gospel. Arnot's stake was a higher one; the riches he sought could not be calculated in dollars, francs, or pounds.

Arnot was also the first man to recognize the strategic importance of this section of Central Africa. The idea was born in his mind of a chain of stations linking the coast with Katanga. All along the way were many tribes speaking many languages, but all virgin soil for the gospel. His far-seeing vision has been realized. A chain of mission centers has been established from Bié in Angola in the west to Elizabethville in the Congo. Both north and south of this line there has been considerable expansion. The area became known as "The Beloved Strip," owing to the number of devoted men and women who have given their lives in making Arnot's vision a reality.

PART II

Ireland and Portugal

Ever since I was a boy, I wanted to be a missionary in Africa. This desire had been awakened and stimulated by reading the life stories of Livingstone, Arnot, and Mary Slessor, and by hearing men home on furlough from the mission field. Frankly I was a hero worshipper. I thought that these were the greatest men of modern times, and longed to follow in their footsteps and see the places where they worked.

I had the inestimable privilege of having Christian parents. The 1859 revival has left permanent marks on the manner of life of the people of Northern Ireland. The people are mostly of Scotch Covenanting stock, God-fearing and Bible-conscious. After the Huguenot massacres in France, many of these persecuted people came to Ulster, bringing their skills with them. Northern Ireland has always been a stronghold of Reformation principles and a fruitful field for gospel preaching. Many of the early Brethren were Irishmen. J. N. Darby, William Kelly, Lord Congleton, James G. Bellett, Dr. Edward Cronin, George F. Trench, all had an Irish background. There are now about one hundred and fifty New Testament assemblies in the six counties of Ulster, with a very practical missionary interest in every part of the world. It was into this atmosphere that the writer was born in Belfast, Northern Ireland, in 1902.

Although born into a Christian home and nurtured in the facts and teachings of the Bible, I knew that I was not a Christian. I was not very old when I realized I was a sinner and needed a new life and a new power to overcome inbred wickedness. In short, I needed to be born anew. Conviction of sin was very real. Resolutions to overcome evil habits and tendencies only ended in failure. A providential escape from sudden death brought on a spiritual crisis. My problem was that I knew all the facts of the gospel and never doubted them. I knew that Christ had died on the cross for sinners such as I, but stumbled at the simplicity of personal faith in the Saviour's work for my salvation.

It was the custom in Ireland for two evangelists to have series of gospel meetings, sometimes lasting for six or eight weeks, in tents or halls or farmers' barns. One night in May 1918 I slipped into the back seat of a little wooden hall in Fulton Street, off Shaftesbury Square in Belfast, where meetings of this type were being held. The preachers were Robert Curran, a young man full of zeal, and an elderly gracious man, Sam Wright. Mr. Curran in the course of his address made a statement that arrested me.

"When Christ died upon the cross," he said, "God His Father was satisfied with the atoning work of His Son, and to prove that, He raised Him from the dead."

I said to myself: "Well if God is satisfied, why should I not be satisfied too?" Then it occurred to me, how do I know that Christ died for me? Almost immediately the words of Isaiah 53:5 came to mind: *"But He was wounded for our transgressions, He was bruised for our iniquities: the chastisement of our peace was upon Him; and with His stripes we are healed."* I bowed my head and said, "Lord, if He was wounded and bruised and chastised for me, I accept Him as my Saviour and Lord."

Joy and peace and the assurance of salvation flooded my soul. I knew I was born again and that the Holy Spirit had come in to dwell. I knew that my salvation did not depend on my feelings, but on what the Saviour had done for me, and I had the assurance of the Word of God that if I trusted in Him, I would have everlasting life. This was the great turning point in my life.

I openly confessed my faith in Christ and a month later was baptized and received into church fellowship in the Donegall

Road assembly in Belfast.

My training for the mission field was almost entirely of a practical kind. I was an apprentice for five years in Harland and Wolf's shipyard, then the largest in the world. The training I received in the use of tools in this place proved invaluable in later years.

Every day a group of men gathered together at the dinner hour in the shipyard for a Bible study session. Some of these were able Bible teachers, eager to help young Christians. Many of the young men who sat on rough planks in that circle are prominent workers on the mission field today in many parts of the world. We studied the great basic doctrines of the New Testament and private study was encouraged by free discussion with men who represented practically every denominational viewpoint.

In the summer time we spent our Saturday afternoons with the "Village Workers." This was a group of young men, led by older experienced businessmen, who systematically covered the whole of Counties Antrim and Down preaching the gospel. We traveled on bicycles, visited every home with literature and an invitation to an open air meeting in the village square. In the evening we had supper together at a restaurant, and then the meeting at some central point. It was here we attempted public speaking for the first time. In those days we knew little about elocution, homiletics, or hermeneutics, but from a full heart told out the message of God's love to men; and blessing resulted. In most of the places visited regularly year by year, a New Testament church functions today, and the work still goes on.

In those days the reading of two books made a permanent impression on my mind. The first was the biography of Hudson Taylor, who was the founder and pioneer of the China Inland Mission. The second was the autobiography of George Muller of Bristol. Here was a man who, for fifty years, was responsible for the maintenance of an orphanage with 2,000 children. He was a man of prayer who never mentioned his needs to anyone but God. Again and again he did not know where the next meal for the children would come from, but God miraculously supplied every need. His life and testimony were a rebuke to religious begging. He was pre-eminently a man of simple faith in a God who answers prayer. Here was guidance for my life. I wanted, if only in a small way, to put these principles into practice.

Fred Lane of Angola came to Belfast in 1921 for a series of missionary conferences. He gave a most graphic description of a pioneer journey he had undertaken to the Bangala tribe in the north of Angola. He told of an area where there were a number of tribes entirely unevangelized and at the same time friendly and wide open to the Christian missionary.

Mr. Lane made no emotional appeal for volunteers, but his quiet reserved manner and straightforward story of a need made a deep impression on my mind, which in time developed into a heavy burden of conviction, that perhaps this was the Lord's plan for my life, and the niche where I might serve. After three years of deep exercise and correspondence with Mr. Lane, my desire to serve the Lord in Africa was finally realized.

In the meantime I had been working hard at language and other studies with a tutor at night. A knowledge of the vocabulary and grammar of the Portuguese language was a help when I later went to Portugal and was a foundation for the study of other languages in Africa.

In 1923 I felt that the time had come to take some definite step in preparation for the mission field. I told my desire to go to Angola to the elders of the assembly in Donegall Road, Belfast, where I was in church fellowship. Although I was only twenty-one years old, they graciously gave me their full co-operation and a letter commending me to the Lord for His work.

At a farewell meeting, when George Gould, a saintly servant of the Lord, was bidding me good-bye, he said: "I have decided to go with you, all the way." When I asked him what he meant, he replied, "I will pray for you every day that you are in Africa." Twenty-three years later, when he was a very old man, I met him again in Chicago. He told me that he had faithfully kept his promise, and all through the years had prayed for me three times a day! Knowing the man and his fragrant life, and his intimacy with the Lord, I was just able to stammer in reply, "Mr. Gould, that explains a tremendous lot."

I left Ireland in October 1923, with a third-class ticket to take me as far as Lisbon in Portugal, but with no passage money beyond that, no supplies, and without a promise of support from anyone. I felt that I wanted simply to trust God from day to day and try honestly to put into practice the principles I had learned from the Bible. As responsibility and correspondence has increased, I have been sorely tempted to resort to the expedient of writing a bimonthly form letter and circulating it among my friends. I have no criticism of many of my esteemed brethren who do this, but I have always had a conscience about it, and have deliberately avoided propaganda and publicity of every kind. I wanted to satisfy myself whether the principle of simple faith in God would work today or not. After over forty years of testing and varied experience, I can gladly testify that it does.

The journey to Portugal occupied four and a half days, calling in at ports in France and Spain. I traveled on a ship which I had helped to build. I was proud to think that I had personally built one of the lifeboats on the boat deck. My cabin mates, in a third-class room under the forecastle, were mostly Spanish speaking, immigrants bound for South America. I had my first taste of olive oil and boiled codfish, and incidentally of seasickness.

In Lisbon no one met me at the boat. I was a stranger in a strange land. I had studied the Portuguese language with a Brazilian teacher before leaving home, but like many another sojourner, I found that the Portuguese of the textbooks is very different from that spoken by the man in the street. I had the address of a missionary who had lived in Lisbon for many years. I crossed the street to a policeman directing traffic, and in my best Portuguese asked him for directions. He did not understand a word of what I said, and in return poured out a torrent of fluent Portuguese which left me breathless.

I wandered up and down the streets, inquiring as I went. I must have given a good deal of amusement to the people I accosted. Lisbon, like Rome, is built on seven hills and that afternoon I must have negotiated every one of them. The heat was intense and I was amused to see the mules and donkeys wearing hats with their ears sticking through holes cut in the brims, to protect them from the intense rays of the sun. At last, thoroughly exhausted, I met a Portuguese who directed me to an English lady. She kindly escorted me to my address and handed me over.

The missionary did not seem overjoyed at my arrival, but was good enough to give me hospitality for the night and next morning took me to a hotel near the docks and helped me to arrange for room and board. It was called "York House" and formerly had been a monastery. My room once had been a monk's cell and had a stone floor.

Next day the missionary came back and offered to help me get my luggage through customs. When I told him that I did not have any luggage liable to customs, he asked me where I was going, how much money I had, and how long I intended to stay in Lisbon. When I answered his questions, he seemed astonished.

"I am an old man and you are a very young man," he said. "I would advise you to take the first boat back to England!" When I got over my shock, I told him that I respected his advice, but that responsible people had commended me to missionary work and that I planned to stay for some time in Portugal and study the language in preparation for going to Africa.

"I think you would be doing more good in Northern Ireland than staying here to study Portuguese," he replied with a shrug of the shoulders. I began to realize that my ideas of trusting God and living by faith were not popular!

In the meantime I settled down to work hard at the language, spending on an average about twelve hours a day in study. I had been informed that in order to get a visa to work in Angola, it would be necessary to pass an examination in Portuguese grade school subjects. Government authorities in Lisbon insisted on this. As well as the Portuguese language, it was necessary to study Portuguese history, geography, their methods of doing arithmetic, elementary science, etc. I hired a competent Portuguese teacher and set to work.

It was winter time and with no heat in my room, with its stone floor, it was dreadfully cold. I took off my shoes, wrapped a sweater round my feet, and tried to forget it. After being in Lisbon for six months I passed the examination and received the certificate. After some years this certificate was exchanged by the Portuguese educational authorities for a diploma authorizing me to teach Portuguese in an elementary school in Africa. But during my many years in Africa, teaching school among other things, no official has ever asked to see it.

It is one thing to have a theoretical knowledge of the vocabulary and grammar of a language, but it is something quite different to be able to use it. I thought it would be helpful in getting fluency in the language, to attempt some gospel meetings. Accordingly I bought some hymnbooks and crossed the River Tagus to a town called Barreiro, where no gospel work of any kind was being carried on. I hired a room at the local hotel and then set out to find a place where I could invite the people for meetings.

This was before the Salazar regime came into power and the place was a hotbed of communists, so I encountered a good deal of ridicule and opposition. One day a cooper making wine casks told me to go and do an honest day's work, in-stead of distributing literature. I took off my coat and picked up his tools. He seemed surprised that I could fit the staves of a barrel together as well as he could, and not only took my books but invited me to stay for a meal.

At last a place was found which would hold about a hundred people. I paid the rent for a month, arranged seating accommodation, and started inviting the people. At first only the children came, but gradually the adults were attracted and a real interest was developing.

One night a gang of communists came in and sat on the back seats wearing their caps. I asked them to remove them while I prayed, but they refused and their general attitude showed that they were out to make trouble. However I went on with the meeting. At the close they came up in a body, started to threaten me, and then one raised his hand to strike me. At that, a man in overalls jumped up, drew a pistol, and dared anyone to lay hands on me. I quickly reached up and turned out the lights, hustled them all into the street, and locked the door. When they dispersed I slipped round to the hotel where I was staying.

Next day the Portuguese administrator sent for me. He pulled open a drawer in his desk and showed me the fragments of a bomb which these same toughs had thrown at somebody the week before. He told me that to insure my safety he would have to prohibit me from having any more meetings. I assured him that I was willing to take the risk, but he refused to reverse his decision. I then asked him if he had any objection to my going to his superiors in Lisbon and asking permission to carry on the meetings. He said that he did not mind, but as far as he was concerned, that was the end of the matter.

Next day I went over to Lisbon, enlisted the help of some Portuguese friends, and had an interview with the governor. He gave us permission in writing to continue the meetings. A nice work developed and, after I left for Africa, it was carried on by Portuguese friends.

Each Saturday I came over to Lisbon from Barreiro for the services at Santa Catarina on Sunday and usually had my meals at Mr. Swan's house in Rua Sao Bento. Mr. Swan was one of the early pioneers in Africa and his home in Lisbon was a rendez-vous for recruits who were studying the Portuguese language with Africa in mind. His living room was full of African curios; buffalo, sable antelope, and other horns were on the walls, and at the door was the huge skull of a hippo, with open jaws and shining teeth, which Swan had shot.

Here for the first time I met Elizabeth D. Smyth from Hartford, Connecticut. She, too, planned to work in Angola. She had been interested in missionary work through the influence of Mary Ridley, a lady who had spent many years in China. But instead of China, Elizabeth decided to give her life to Africa. We became good friends in the short time we were together in Portugal. In those days I had the idea that a pioneer missionary should remain unmarried and should not allow himself to be hampered by the responsibilities of a wife and home. Later on I changed my mind!

Friends in Ireland sent gifts of money from time to time. Some of these were from humble people who gave at considerable sacrifice to themselves. One gift at this time was from a Portuguese Christian friend in Lisbon and was particularly heart-warming. He had been recently married and was starting a hardware business. He gave me 500 escudos with a little note to the effect that he wanted to start his married life by giving to the Lord for His work. At that time a clerk in business earned about 500 escudos a month, so that actually he was giving me a month's pay!

After ten months in Portugal, I felt that the time had come to leave for Africa. All my needs had been supplied and I did not owe anyone anything. One day in counting my money, I found that I had sufficient to buy a third-class ticket on a Portuguese ship bound for Angola. The cost was about $45.00 at the present rate of exchange. After buying the ticket I had a little left over to buy some necessary articles of outfit. I had a sailmaker make me a small canvas tent. Then I bought a collapsible cot bed. The last item was a case of one hundred tins of sardines. I had heard that the Africans' staple diet was corn meal mush, and I thought that the sardines would at least make it palatable!

The day before I left Portugal an incident happened that was a great encouragement. Some friends in Ireland sent me a post office money order for £24. On sailing day I took this to the post office and the clerk cashed it in Portuguese currency. At that time the currency was very unstable and the exchange had soared to 150 escudos to the pound. In normal times it had been five to the pound. They had only notes of small denomination in the post office and I received a large parcel of money for my £24. When I arrived at the ship, I was allotted to a large cabin under the forecastle in which ten men were to sleep. Two of these were *degredados* (criminals) going out to Africa to complete a sentence for crimes committed in Portugal. They were being escorted by two soldiers. The other five in the cabin were Portuguese peasants. When I saw my traveling companions, I began to feel anxious about my parcel of money, which in the cramped quarters was practically impossible to conceal.

In three days we reached Madeira. I went ashore with my money and explained my problem to the manager of the bank. He changed my money back into English currency, charging me a small discount. On the fifteenth day out from Lisbon we reached Luanda, the capital of Angola. I went ashore again and met an Irish Methodist missionary, Robert Shields. He was very kind and hospitable, gave me some valuable advice, and then asked if he could help me to exchange my money. He introduced me to a German trader who changed my £24 into Portuguese currency at the rate of 220 escudos to the pound. He too had notes of small denomination, and by the time he finished counting my little pile had increased about 40 percent.

Nothing was further from my mind than gambling on the money market, but it so happened that on the day I landed, the exchange had soared to its peak and then started to go down. Shortly afterwards the currency was stabilized at 100 escudos to the pound and later at 80, where it remains today. In any case, God saw my need and I had sufficient to pay my way through customs at Lobito and for subsequent expenses on the journey upcountry.

Some of my friends had strongly advised me against traveling third class on a Portuguese ship. But I had no alternative. Actually conditions were not as bad as I had imagined. The bunk was clean and the food abundant, but it was the kind suited to a Portuguese laboring man, plenty of rice and beans mixed with cubes of fat pork and tripe. Instead of water or tea, we were served sour wine at each meal. I refused the wine but always had plenty to eat. The Portuguese always were delighted when there was *"bacalhão corn batatas"* on the menu. This was boiled codfish and potatoes soaked with olive oil and vinegar. They always came back for second helpings.

On the eighteenth day out from Lisbon we sighted Lobito, our destination on the West African Coast.

First Impressions of Angola

When I landed at Lobito in 1924 it was still undeveloped. There was only one primitive "hotel," infested with bugs and cockroaches and no modern plumbing. I slept on a table the two nights I was there; it would have been more comfortable sleeping on the warm sand outside. In spite of the primitive conditions and the terrific heat, the Portuguese proprietor of the hotel, a stickler for convention, insisted that we wear ties and jackets at the table!

Nearby, at Benguela, was the spot where the early missionaries had landed and where some of them had died before their work commenced. It was also the terminus of the old slave path from the interior. On the other side of the bay I could see the narrow path on which they had walked, winding down the mountainside. The mud-brick compounds in which they had been confined were still in existence. Benguela has not much changed; old rusty cannon sticking out of the sand beside the ancient fort were reminders of its long sad history, and swarthy pockmarked Portuguese old-timers, dozing in the sun on the sidewalk outside the cafés, proclaimed the fact that modern development had passed them by.

But here at last I had my feet on African soil, the ambitions of many years realized. As I thought of the unknown future in the interior of Africa I prayed, "O Lord, give me three years and I will be satisfied!"

The train for the interior ran only once a week. Construction of the line ended at Silva Porto, about 350 miles from Lobito. As there was no sleeping berth available, I slept on a pile of luggage in the corridor. After leaving the coast, the train climbs steeply to the top of a mountain range which fringes the coastline. It rises 5,000 feet above sea level in about 100 miles. At one point there is a third rail in the middle of the track, with a ratchet-like device under the chassis of the locomotive, which prevents it running back in the event of a failure of power! As there is no coal in the country, the locomotives burn firewood. Plantations of eucalyptus trees have been planted along the line to insure a future supply of fuel. After reaching the high altitude of the plateau, the weather turned suddenly cold, especially at night. I noticed that some of the Africans at the stations along the line were wearing potato sacks with holes cut out for their heads and arms. All were barefooted and any who wore a battered hat took it off respectfully when a white man passed.

The journey to Silva Porto occupied two nights and a day. This is a historic spot named for the famous Portuguese explorer and trader who befriended F. S. Arnot and who brought him to Angola in 1885 from the Zambesi. His old homestead, a short distance from the modern town, is now preserved as a museum.

I was met at Silva Porto by William Maitland, the veteran pioneer to the Chokwe tribe. He was a quiet, reserved, slow-spoken Irishman with snow-white hair. As he extended his hand, he simply said: "Welcome to Africa," and then introduced me to some of the Chokwe-speaking Africans whom he had brought with him from the interior. I was surprised to hear them speak quite good Portuguese.

Maitland traveled in a Reo Speed Wagon of which he was very proud. It was one of the first automobiles in the country and was a pioneer, too, in every sense of the word. The wheels had wooden spokes, and on more than one occasion when, traversing rough country, a wheel went to pieces, Maitland sat by the wayside and laboriously whittled and fitted new spokes, with a native ax and a penknife as his only tools. He carried some pieces of seasoned wood in his toolbox under the seat for this purpose.

We shall meet the Reo Speed Wagon again later on. On this occasion it brought me to my destination at Chilonda, a mission station among the Umbundu-speaking people in Bié, over a rutted dirt road full of potholes, about 25 miles from Silva Porto. On the way we crashed into a deep hole filled with water and broke one of the rear springs. Temporary repairs were made by the roadside in the dark. We limped into Chilonda with the spring tied up with oxhide thongs. On the way we passed Kuanjululu, the site of the first mission station in this area. Here Arnot had located in 1889, but for various reasons the station had been later moved to Chilonda, about 10 miles away.

In the early days, avenues of eucalyptus trees had been planted at Chilonda. These were regarded as a disinfectant of the air against the deadly Anopheles mosquito which carries malaria. The trees had grown to a tremendous height and girth, some of them eight feet in diameter at the base.

The houses were all built of adobe sun-dried brick, thatched with grass, and with clay floors. The floors were covered with bamboo mats woven with strips of black bark. The only lighting was kerosene lamps suspended by a wire from a roof beam. None of the houses or rooms were ceiled. The walls were plastered with mud and whitewashed with a white clay. Furniture was all handmade.

I spent my first week in a little one-roomed house which had been built by Mr. Arnot and where he had stayed when he was at Chilonda. I was introduced to a mosquito net for the first time. This was tied by a rope from one of the roof beams and hung like a tent over the bed. At sundown, the ends were tucked under the mattress. As well as this, I was advised to take five grains of quinine every day as a prophylactic against malaria.

The mattress was not a "Beautyrest" model imported from America, but consisted of a calico bag filled with cornhusks. This was laid on a bamboo mat stretched across wooden slats on the framework of the bed. The pillow was stuffed with soft white thistledown from a bullrush-like plant which grew in the swamps. Everything was spotlessly clean and felt good after what I had grown accustomed to in Portugal and on the journey out.

In 1924 when I arrived at Chilonda, Edward Sanders was the senior missionary there. He was an Englishman from Liverpool, who before coming to Africa had been a chemist. He had come out to help Arnot in 1897. After a short spell at Cavungu, near the Angolan border of Northern Rhodesia, now Zambia, he came back to Chilonda, where he spent fifty years of faithful service. He, too, like Maitland, was a soft-spoken, retiring type of man. He had a florid complexion and a large white handle-barred mustache which made him look like a retired Indian army general. He had a highly developed sense of humor and loved to tell jokes which some thought were saved up in a scrapbook. He was an expert gardener with a large citrus orchard, where he experimented with grafting and budding trees. Most missions and many of the traders and government officials in the country benefited from his experience, as he distributed thousands of lemon, orange, grapefruit, and tangerine trees all over the country. This was a highly valuable service in a tropical country where fresh fruit was unobtainable.

Chilonda was a stopping place for the slave caravans from the interior to the coast. Many thousands of these poor unfortunates had passed through the place during the first decade of this century on their way to Benguela. Sanders had a compound as a home for little girls whom he had redeemed from this vile traffic; it was still in existence when I arrived there. Many of the people living at Chilonda were formerly slaves whom the missionaries had rescued.

The language spoken at Chilonda is Umbundu. It is a soft, musical Bantu language of the Ovimbundu people, who number about a million and a half. They live in the district of Bié and are sometimes called Biheans.

African
Elders and Preachers

The African has the greatest respect for old age. On coming into the presence of a chief, he gets down on his knees and performs an elaborate ceremony, bowing down till his head touches the dust, then a ritual of hand clapping and the use of respectful terms of address. An elder is called an *osekulu*. The word is used not only for the ruling elders of a village in their tribal life, but it is also the term used for an elder in the church. The whole idea of respect for authority and mature experience is inbred in the African.

When I first arrived at Chilonda, there were three out-standing African elders in the church, Vongula, Sanji, and Sawimbu. The first time I attended a service in the Umbundu language, Vongula was the speaker.

The church building , like the missionaries' homes, was made of sun-dried bricks, plastered with mud and white-washed. It was thatched with grass and had no ceiling. Two kerosene lamps hung by a wire from a roof beam. It had a clay floor with rough plank seats without backs, raised about a foot from the floor. All the men sat on one side and the women on the other. The elders sat on special seats flanking the speaker on the platform. The singing was beautiful. Little children in the front seats harmonized in a delightful way and I could hear rich bass voices of young men at the back. It was easy to see that this was a musical people.

When Vongula rose to speak, I noticed that he was dressed in an old pair of blue pajamas with gold braid. Where buttons were missing, and to hide the fact that he did not have an undershirt, it was pinned at the neck with a safety pin. As he passed me going to the desk, I saw that he was in his bare feet and that there were large thick calluses on his heels, black and cracked. I had never seen a preacher like this before! But as soon as he started to speak and got warmed up to his subject, I forgot about his appearance. Here was an accomplished orator, but more than a mere orator, a man of God. After the service, I asked Sanders about the calluses on Vongula's feet.

"Don't laugh at him," he replied, "those are honorable calluses; that man has literally walked thousands of miles backwards and forwards across Central Africa preaching the gospel." I have often thought that Vongula was a perfect illustration of the passage in Isaiah 52:7, and quoted by Paul in Romans 10:15: *"How beautiful upon the mountains are the feet of him that bringeth good tidings, that publisheth peace"*—the beautiful feet of the Saviour and of the pioneer preacher.

Many years later I met Vongula returning from one of his long journeys into the interior. A little boy carried his bundle of simple belongings, a grass sleeping mat, a tin plate and spoon, and a change of shirt. They had been sleeping on the ground at night beside a fire and eating whatever was set before them by hospitable and friendly Africans. He was carrying a long staff covered from top to bottom with notches cut with a knife. I asked him about the notches.

"In the olden days," he explained, "when I went hunting and shot an animal, I cut a notch on my bow or my gun, and also attached a piece of its hide. Now I am hunting for souls and when one of my people confesses Christ as Saviour, I make a mark on my staff." His staff was covered with them! He never owned a pair of shoes, his large spread-out toes wouldn't have fitted into them anyway, but he was a real evangelist and an honored servant of God. He was the prototype of many African pioneers who in the early days per-formed incredible feats of walking and at the same time gossiped the gospel among their own people.

Sanji, another Chilonda elder, I learned, was one of the first converts in Central Africa. In later years he was tall, lean, white-haired, dignified, independent, with a razor-keen wit. As a lad he went into Lubaland with a caravan of Ovimbundu rubber and slave traders. When he got to Nana Candundu in the Lu-vale country he came down with smallpox. His companions abandoned him, thinking he would die. The missionaries had just arrived in the vicinity and Jeanie Gilchrist from Scotland, hearing of the stricken lad, had a grass hut built, carried him into it, and at some risk to herself, tenderly cared for him until he recovered. On first coming to Angola in 1889, Miss Gilchrist had spent two years in Bié and so knew Sanji's language. Day after day she told him the gospel; he drank it in and was truly converted. He never forgot the gallantry and kindness of the white woman who risked her life to save him, when he had been abandoned by his own people. On returning to Bié, he de-termined to preach the gospel in the village where he was born. But a callow youth is seldom allowed to express his opinion in the presence of his elders. Night after night in the *onjango* (palaver house) he attempted to introduce the subject, but was always rebuffed by the *akulu* (elders). Finally one night he saw his opportunity and told them this story:

"One time in our country there was a severe drought. It hadn't rained for many moons, rivers and lakes had dried up, and many were dying of thirst. The animals of the forest gath-ered to consider what they would do. The first to speak was the lion. He as king demanded obedience from the rest.

"'I know where there is water,' he said. 'If you follow me, I will lead you to the perpetual spring where I drank when I was a cub.'

"When he had finished speaking, the tortoise crawled into the circle and lifting his head, said, 'I know where there is wa-ter!' The lion was so angered at his insolence that he cuffed him with his great paw, but he rolled with the punch and so was not hurt. That day they all followed the lion, but after a long weary journey, when they got to the so-called perpetual spring, lo, it was dry.

"Next day they gathered again, and this time it was the elephant's turn to speak. 'Listen to me,' he bellowed, 'when I was young, and there was a drought, the leader of the herd, a wise old elephant, always took us to a waterhole where the water never dried up. If you follow me, I will take you to that waterhole.'

"When he finished speaking, the tortoise waddled in again and piped up, 'I know where there is water!' The elephant was so mad that he stepped on him with his great foot, but the sand was deep and he sank into it and wasn't squashed. That day they followed the elephant, but when they came to the waterhole it was bone dry, with gaping cracks on the surface. Weary and tired they had to retrace their steps.

"Next day it was the leopard's turn; and then the buffalo's. Even the hyena had his say. Each day the tortoise came with his little speech, 'I know where there is water.'

"Finally disillusioned and discouraged and when they had come to the end of their resources, brother rabbit spoke up.

"'Dear friends,' he declared, 'we have listened very respectfully to our leaders and have loyally followed their advice, but we have been disappointed and are weary and tired and very thirsty. I would suggest that for once we should give brother tortoise a chance and see whether he knows what he is talking about or not.'

"It was all very humiliating, but they were all so thirsty, that they decided to follow tortoise for once, anyway. With tortoise out front, behind came lion and elephant and leopard and buffalo. After a long journey he led them to a lovely bubbling spring that came out of the rock. They all drank and were refreshed and satisfied, and from that time tortoise had the gratitude and thanks of all."

Sanji ended his story with the obvious application. He said, "We have been following you elders for a long time along the dark paths of witchcraft and fear and death and we are thirsty still. But," he ended dramatically, "I know where there is living water!"

He was remarkably successful as an evangelist. In a gospel

service, I heard him describing sin. He used one illustration after another to liven up his various points. His final word was on the universality of sin. He ended with a flourish.

"Why," he said, "it's just like lice, we all have it!" No one in the audience even smiled. They must have thought it was very apt!

On one occasion, a lady in England, hearing of the fine work Sanji was doing, offered to pay him a salary, so that he could give all his time to the work. Sanji asked Mr. Swan, through whom the offer had come, how he was supported. Mr. Swan told him that he had no salary, but looked to the Lord to supply his daily needs. Sanji asked for a day or two to think about the offer. He was a good hunter. He asked the Lord if He wished him to carry on the work the way he had always done, in dependence on Himself, that He would give some definite sign. The next morning he went out with his gun. He had hardly left the village when a duiker jumped out of the grass. He dropped it with his first shot. He took this as a token from the Lord that He would continue to care for him. He then went back to Mr. Swan and told him to write to the lady thanking her for her offer, but that he wished to continue on, looking to the Lord for his support.

Sawimbu was a real pastor in the New Testament sense of the term. I knew him only in later life, when he was an old man. He was reserved and quiet-spoken with an ample re-serve of practical wisdom. Mr. Sanders told me that Sawimbu was mainly responsible for the decision of what attitude to take to polygamy among African people. This was one of the great difficulties in the early days of missionary work. From time immemorial it was the custom for Africans to have more wives than one. Some of the great chiefs had hundreds. A single woman was practically unknown, unless she was an imbecile or a hopeless cripple.

It presented a problem to the missionaries when a man with a number of wives became a Christian and presented himself for church membership. Even the missionaries were divided in their judgment as to how the matter was to be decided. At a conference the matter was being discussed. Some argued that it would be unreasonable to expect a higher standard from primitive Africans, than, for instance, from Abraham, Jacob, or David, who were polygamists. Others inferred from the statement in 1 Timothy 3:2, *"the husband of one wife,"* that an ordinary church member might be a polygamist, but an elder must be the husband of one wife.

After much discussion, Sawimbu quietly arose and said, "Brothers, I think you have all forgotten what the Lord Jesus said about this matter. He said in Matthew 19: *'From the be-ginning it was not so. At the beginning, He made them male and female, and for this cause shall a man leave his father and his mother and shall cleave unto his wife: and they two shall be one flesh.'* Brothers, if one is thirsty and desires a drink of clear pure water, he does not go away downstream where the water has been befouled by men and by the feet of animals, but rather to the head of the stream, where it comes bubbling out of the source. I would suggest that in deciding this matter we should not go to Abraham or Jacob or David, but right back to the fountainhead." That settled the argument. Since then in Bié, and, for that matter, in most places in Central Africa, church membership is limited to those with one wife and with a clean testimony in their marriage relationships.

At Chilonda there lived a man called Jamba-ye-mina ("pregnant elephant") whom I came to know and respect. When one of the Sanders children was born, there was no milk for the baby. It was the time of the Bailundu war and the whole country was in an uproar. At Benguela, at the coast, was a box of condensed milk which the Sanders badly needed. Jamba-ye-mina volunteered to go for it. He walked the 350 miles to the coast and on the way down and back had to run the gauntlet of the war parties around Bailundu. But he finally made it and saved the day by delivering the milk. He did not think that there was anything extraordinary in the fact that he had walked about 700 miles and carried a 60-pound load on his head half that distance, so that a missionary's baby could have the food it needed.

Capango and Hualondo

After a short time at Chilonda, I went to another mission station called Capango, which is about 40 miles to the northeast. Altogether the Brethren have four mission stations in Bié among the Umbundu-speaking people. This would be in an area about the size of Connecticut. Chilonda is the oldest, being founded in 1892; Hualondo, 1893; Capango, 1905; and Chitau, 1920. The American Board (A.B.C.F.M.) was working in Bié to the south and west, but there was no overlapping or competition.

Capango was started by Fred Lane as a branch work from Chilonda. It later developed into a main center. Mr. Lane was one of the early pioneers in Garenganze and was a most gracious, kindly man. It was through him that I was first of all attracted to Africa. He was a great walker and a crack shot. He loved the African and was never happier than when telling out the gospel at the campfire, after tramping 20 miles during the day. When I arrived, he was designing a new meeting room to seat a thousand people. In those days it was impossible to get burnt roof tiles or cement, so it was built entirely of adobe brick with a grass roof. But it was beautifully done and served its purpose for forty years. The roof was supported by hardwood pillars. Being young and agile and accustomed to working at considerable heights in the shipyard, I had the job of helping to erect the roof timbers. Mr. Lane was a perfectionist and the building was a credit to him.

It was at Capango that 1 first met Annie Gammon, who had been there since 1905. She came from a well-known missionary family who lived at Ilfracombe in the South of England. She often told us that she trusted Christ for salvation when she was four years of age. As a child she sat on the knee of Robert C. Chapman, the patriarch of Barnstable. At least five members of her family came to Africa as missionaries.

But there was one matter which gave me a good deal of concern. The mission station was run as a "Christian village." When an African was converted he usually left his own environment, built a house on the mission station, and isolated himself from his old life. There was a strict code of laws on the station which covered practically every phase of his life. The missionary's word was law and was carried out by an elder called an *osekulu*. If a resident on the mission station committed adultery or broke one of the laws of the village, he was not only disciplined by the local church, but he also had to leave his home and garden and go back into "the world." There were instances where young people had to leave the home of their parents and go and live with heathen relatives. This, I felt, was a wrong principle, but being young I kept my misgivings to myself. I should say that this idea has long since passed away, but it was the rule for many years.

The mission station was run in much the same way that John Calvin ruled Geneva. Calvin had the idea that a city should be governed after the same model as the Israelite theocracy under Moses and Aaron. It was the union of church and state with a vengeance. His severe theological views and blue laws were imposed on people by force, whether they were church members or not. The remorseless logic of this policy led to the burning of Servetus at the stake.

I have felt for many years that, in a pagan country like Central Africa, it is unwise policy to isolate converts to Christianity from their own people. In doing so, they are spared persecution, but they are brought into a hothouse environment where healthy development is retarded. It is not good for the foreigner either.

He is liable to get an exaggerated idea of his own importance. Recent independence movements in practically every part of Africa have proved that the principle of the missionary's building up a work around himself was wrong from the beginning. Sooner or later there is bound to be a reaction. Experience has shown that when the African is encouraged to accept responsibility from the commencement of his Christian life, he develops more naturally, and the work is on a much more solid foundation.

One day Mr. Lane suggested to me that there was a need at a mission station called Hualondo, and that I might be able to help out there. It had been started many years before by George Murrain, a colored missionary from British Guiana. Murrain had recently died after an operation in America, and the work was being carried on by a young Englishman and his wife, Mr. and Mrs. Lance Adcock. He was not too well and was thinking of going home on furlough, but did not want to go unless there was someone to care for the work at Hualondo. Consequently I went over there and settled in. Adcock was very keen on educational work, was a disciplinarian, and a very clever linguist. He suggested that I help in the school, and while I had little liking or fitness for school teaching, I was glad of the opportunity for contact with the people. A Scripture lesson every day in Umbundu, which Adcock took, was a great help to me in learning the language. I lived at Hualondo for eighteen months. After the Adcocks went home to England, I was some months alone on the place. Here I made my first attempts at preaching in the Umbundu language.

An incident occurred here which was a great encouragement in showing God's loving care for material needs. I was living in an adobe brick guest room which had belonged to the Murrains. It had a clay floor covered with bamboo mats and a homemade bed in the middle of the room. On the wall were some pegs, and all the clothes I had in the world, except what I was wearing, were hanging on the pegs. In the corner was a homemade desk where I kept my money, papers, and correspondence.

One night, while I was out at the prayer meeting, an African burgled the place. He first tried to pry open the window with the blade of his ax, but I had secured it with screws from the inside and he failed to open it. He then tried the lock. He put a plug of tobacco against it to deaden the sound, and broke it with blows from his ax. He then went in and plundered the room. When I came back from the prayer meeting, I found the bed stripped and the clothes and the contents of the desk gone. I was practically left in the middle of Africa with the clothes I was standing up in. The next day, the man who did it came and clucked with his tongue and sympathized with me in my loss. It was only two years later that I found out he was the culprit! I felt pretty miserable. In those days it was not easy to get supplies in the country, but I tried to be as philosophical about it as I could.

A couple of weeks later an African turned up with a large bundle on his head. It was sewn up in cloth and had been sent on from the railhead in Silva Porto. When I opened it, I found sheets, pillow cases, clothing, and underwear, and in the center a letter from some ladies in Belfast, Ireland. It contained money which they said was to defray customs on the parcel and they hoped the contents would prove useful! On examining the datestamp, I found it had been sent off a couple of months before the robbery happened. It had been beautifully timed, and here was everything duplicated and brand new!

The Chokwes are expert hunters and never returned to camp empty-handed. Each morning we were presented with a leg of venison. We cooked a few slices and gave the rest back to the men. They finished every scrap every night.

"Our honeymoon walk of thirteen days took us to our little three-roomed mud-and-wattle house…with four bare walls, a grass roof, and clay floor. We slept in a tent for nearly six months, while I made doors and windows to make the little house habitable.

The bushcar was practical on the tortuous 9-inch paths through the forest. When the road was good, Africans could run about eight miles an hour.

Gathering at the waterhole for a baptism at six in the morning, the place seemed black with people, fully two thousand strong.

PART III

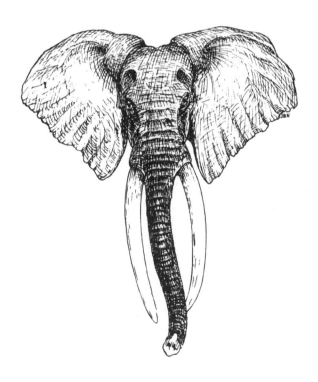

Language Study

The primary task of a foreign missionary is to learn the language of the people. Traders and tourists may "pick up the lingo," but the man or woman who wants to reach the hearts of the people with the Word of life must have a thorough, accurate knowledge of their language. It takes years of hard work, and even at the end of a lifetime, the expert is always learning something new.

Babel may have commenced in ancient Assyria but it has reached its greatest chaos in modern Africa. Years ago a linguistic survey revealed 843 languages and dialects in Africa. The figure is probably an understatement. An ethnographic survey has given the names and location of about 3,000 tribes and subtribes. Many of these never had their languages or dialects investigated by capable linguists. About one third of the population probably has become so used to some of the great languages, such as Arabic, Hausa, Swahili, as to feel as much at home in them as with their original speech.

Of the 250 African languages already reduced to writing, about 200 are the product of Protestant missionaries. The missionary translator reverses the curse of Babel and invokes the blessing of Pentecost.

Africans as a rule are splendid linguists. Even children are taught to speak properly and seldom slip up on a verb tense. Most of the men are bilingual and many are trilingual. We often meet Bantu tribesmen who cannot read a line but can speak five or six African dialects fluently. It is a common mistake of the white man to imagine that savage folk use crude elementary forms of speech. Many African languages are far more precise and more beautifully formed than English. It is a mystery how they have been developed and systematized over the centuries.

I had spent nearly a year in Portugal getting a working knowledge of the Portuguese language. This is the government language of Angola, used for all correspondence with official-dom. Then an important part of our missionary work was teaching school, and this had to be done in the Portuguese language. The law forbids the use of any other language in school. It is the policy of the authorities to latinize the Africans, make them into Portuguese citizens, speaking their language and adopting their culture. All education is therefore in the Portuguese language, the African languages being deliberately suppressed. The argument is that the task of translation into so many native dialects is impossible and a waste of time, as they will tend to die out anyway. I have heard an official, who spoke no language but his own, call a beautiful African tongue "monkey language" only fit for animals. This was because he had never taken the trouble to study it. But who has the right to suppress or destroy the mother tongue of any people?

My first task in Angola was to learn the Umbundu language. This was spoken by the African people in Bié, among whom I lived. It is used by about a million people on the plateau stretching from Lobito at the coast to the Quanza River about 350 miles inland. Early missionaries of the American Congregational Board had committed the language to writing and there was a good-sized vocabulary compiled by one of their missionaries, a Mr. Fay, with a very primitive and sketchy grammar. In those days there were no organized language schools or teachers and, apart from these helps, I had to learn by personal contact with the Africans. Perhaps this was just as well, as most foreigners are liable to keep their American or British intonation, and this with an Irish brogue thrown in would be a queer mixture! An Ochimbundu boy, called Ngongo, came every day and helped with conversation and pronunciation.

The pioneers who first committed African languages to writing had a formidable task. There is nothing in common between African and European languages. But one happy decision was made: to use the Roman alphabet and to write phonetically, that is, to write the words as they sounded. We are thankful today that we did not have to master a script like Chinese or Arabic.

But there is the danger of oversimplification. One African language (Zulu), for instance, contains seven simple vowel sounds, four diphthongs, thirty-six elementary consonant sounds, and nine click consonants—a total of sixty-three sounds, without counting various modifications. How are these to be represented by the twenty-six letters of the English alphabet? Our Roman alphabet, as it stands, does not meet the need of every language, because it does not contain sufficient letters. There are two ways of overcoming this difficulty: either to invent new letters or else to use a system of diacritical signs above or below the existing letters to indicate the new sounds. Actually both methods are used in the languages spoken in Angola.

In attempting to learn the Umbundu language, I often look back with a shiver and a blush at the atrocious mistakes I made. The African has a highly developed sense of humor, but he listened to these blunders politely with a deadpan expression on his face. Some of the young girls giggle, but the men control their emotions until later, when, in the absence of the missionary, the blunders are repeated around the campfire to the accompaniment of howls of laughter.

Four things are necessary in learning a language. First of all, to have a good working knowledge of the grammar of one's own language. It seems foolish for one to attempt to master a foreign tongue when he doesn't know his own. Secondly, it is important to have a good musical ear to distinguish differences in tone. A deaf person would have difficulty in mastering a language. Thirdly, one must have a good memory to retain what he hears. Fourthly, one should be something of a mimic to reproduce what is heard. Some training in phonetics is useful, but experience has shown that the best linguists are those with these four qualifications, who really apply themselves.

Constant contact with the people in their daily life is necessary over a period of time. I always carried a notebook and pencil to note down new words, idiomatic phrases, and proverbs as I heard them. These had to be checked and rechecked to get their real meaning. An African usually quotes just the first words of a proverb, because the audience knows the rest. For instance: A bird in the hand! Or a rolling stone!

In Bantu languages the important word is the noun. There is a system of noun classes, each class with a different prefix. This prefix is attached to each word in the sentence. For in-stance, in the Umbundu language the word for "house" is *onjo* and the prefix is *yi*. "My house is small" would be *onjo yange yitito*. Some African languages have as many as fifteen noun classes, each with a different prefix for the singular and plural. In Umbundu the word for one person is *Ochimbundu* and the plural, *Ovimbundu*, is the name of the tribe. The first syllable is changed to alter the meaning of the word. Thus words are inflected, conjugated, or defined by this system of prefixes. A missionary in Uganda says that the best definition of Bantu languages he ever heard was given by an Irishman: "Bantu languages are those that have their termination at the beginning."

Then the verbs are more precise and complex than in English. The Chokwe language, for instance, has eighteen distinct tenses or variations of the verb. To illustrate: the verb "to do" is *ku-linga*. The past tense has the following: *hi na chi linga*—"I have done it just now." *Ha chi linga*—"I have done it recently." *Na chi linganga*—"I did it this morning." *Ngu na ka chi linga*—"I did it yesterday." *Na chi lingile*—the plain past definite tense. *Na ka chi lingile*—the historic past. No adverb of time is used, a simple verb tense indicates when the action took place. As well as this, there are compound tenses. It is amazing to see a man in his bare feet and a loincloth using with fluency and accuracy a language as precise as this.

There are of course certain lacks and deficiencies. They do not have the technical vocabulary that we have, and they do not have terms to describe things they have never seen, snow, for instance. It is difficult to find suitable words to translate accurately abstract terms as are found in the Bible. "Holiness," "sanctification," and even a generic word for "sin," is not easy to find. In some cases approximations have to be used and the people educated to understand their full meaning.

Another lack is in the names for different shades of color. They have names for black, white, and red, but no real words for gray or pink or green. They do not seem to appreciate the beauty and variations of color as we do. I have never heard an African express any admiration for the beauty of a sunrise or the glory of the sunset. They are afraid of the rainbow, believing that if the end of it touches them, they will die. They have never heard of the pot of gold said to be at its foot!

Ngongo, my language teacher, could read and write, but he could not explain the fine points of grammar or conjugate a verb. His chief function was to tell me the names of things and correct my pronunciation. He spoke fairly good Portuguese. When I made a mistake, he would patiently explain in Portuguese. As time went on and Umbundu became more familiar, he dropped Portuguese entirely and used his own language.

Every day I brought him a list of words which I had heard in conversation. He spent hours trying to teach me the high and low tones of certain vowels. If the wrong tone were used, it would completely alter the meaning of the word. Grammar I had to learn the hard way by listening and noting the way verbs were used. It took about six months' study for me to be able to carry on a conversation with an African and about a year before I could preach with any degree of liberty in Umbundu.

Early attempts at preaching were weak affairs. I wrote out my entire message in Umbundu, Ngongo corrected it and made suggestions, then I memorized it and tried to deliver it without notes. Mr. Adcock, my fellow missionary, was a great help, too. He spoke beautiful Umbundu and I learned a lot from listening to him, but he was usually too busy to give me lessons, so I was left mostly to Ngongo and my own efforts. Now, after forty years' contact with the language, I admit that it is a lifetime task. Very few white men get behind the black man's mind and are able to "think black."

The African loves to use proverbs; ordinary speech among the people is often interlarded with them. Here is a translation of a few of them.

A beetle is a beauty in the eyes of its mother.
There is no beast that does not roar in its own den.
The hunchback is never told to stand upright.
Baboons laugh at the ugliness of each other.
A peacemaker often receives blows.
Two crocodiles cannot live in one hole.
The partridge loves peas, but not those that go
with it into the pot.

We have sometimes heard prospective missionaries, who have had no experience outside their own land, announce publicly that they are going to Africa to translate the Bible. This is a worthy ambition and any training in linguistics before coming to the field is valuable, but older missionaries listen to the statements sometimes made by recruits with mixed feelings.

We quote from Dr. Eugene Nida, the translation secretary of the American Bible Society:

"No Bible translation should be done in a language until the missionary translator is able to discuss freely in the native language all the problems of form and meaning...In one mission in Africa, it was the normal practice to assign new missionaries, after three months of preliminary language work, to the task of Bible translating. The work was done with native informants but the results were, of course, just word-for-word renderings. These initial efforts were fortunately revised before being submitted for publication, but such work should have been thrown away and a fresh start made, for it proved impossible to 'weed out' of these original immature translations the highly artificial and almost meaningless phrases and sentences."

These are wise words and should be carefully pondered by would-be translators. Usually translation work is under-taken by men of long experience who know the African mind and the idiom of the language, as well as a wide and accurate knowledge of the Word of God. It is not a task for the novice.

The Unevangelized North

My object in coming to Angola was to work in unevangelized territory. My imagination had been fired by Mr. Lane's stories of vast regions in the north of Angola, with pagan tribes waiting for the gospel. The Bangala tribe especially was on my heart. I determined as soon as possible to pay them a visit and find out if it would be possible to find a place where I could build a house, learn their language, and settle among them. I discussed the matter with Mr. Adcock, with whom I was living at Hualondo. He shared my views about pioneer evangelism and we decided to go together. There were no roads in the area to which we were going, so the journey meant a walk of 540 miles and occupied five weeks. We walked on an average of about 20 miles a day and slept at night near a native village or beside a stream. We started off at the end of April 1925.

Everything we needed for the journey we had to take with us. We had no difficulty in getting men to carry our loads. An African porter can carry a sixty-pound load. On top of this he has a few personal belongings, a grass sleeping mat, a cotton blanket, a cooking pot, and his native ax. Some take along a bow and arrows also. Each man has a goatskin bag in which he carries either corn or cassava meal for making his evening meal of mush. Usually they have only one meal a day, in the evening.

Before leaving camp in the morning, they may have a couple of roasted sweet potatoes or a cob of corn, but the big meal of the day is at night, cooked over the open campfire.

Altogether we had fifteen men. We had a tent eight feet square in which to sleep. This with the tent poles was a two-man load. No one wanted to carry the tent, because if it rained it would weigh twice as much. Then we had a food box which contained some tinned meat and fish, flour, sugar, ingredients for making pancakes or bread, and a cake and tins of cookies which we tried to ration out as long as we could. There was usually a rush of volunteers to carry the food box, since it got lighter as we went along! Then each of us had a bed load, consisting of a large canvas kit bag, with a collapsible cot bed, some blankets, a pillow, waterproof ground sheet, and a canvas washhand basin. The cook boy had a lighter load of pots and pans and an empty gasoline can in which to draw water for cooking and washing. These gasoline cans were invaluable and were used for all kinds of purposes.

As well as personal needs, we took along a couple of loads of salt. This was for barter. The people have a special word for salt hunger and, in the interior, anything the people had could be bought with it. Nothing would please a child more than to put a spoonful of salt on his tongue. They sucked it like candy. In the native villages, as we went along, we bought eggs, mushrooms, corn, and sweet potatoes with salt. There was a recognized scale of barter. A cup of salt was worth three eggs, and so on. The salt came from the coast. Sea water was evaporated on the hard flats at Lobito and Benguela, the salt swept up along with the dirt, and sent up country for sale. It was a valuable commodity.

The usual contract with the porters was that they would be responsible for their food on the way out, but we would be responsible for the return journey. The men were paid either with cloth or Portuguese cash. Most of them wanted cloth. This was a trade calico which came from Manchester in England. Over the years, when Portuguese taxes, which each man had to pay, became heavier, the people wanted pay in money and trade cloth fell into disuse.

When each man had received his load, he tied two sticks about six feet long, one on either side of it, in such a way that about three feet of the sticks projected beyond the end of the load. These were pulled together into a point and tied. The load was carried on top of his head with the projecting sticks pointing ahead. When the porter wanted to rest, he simply bowed his head until the sticks touched the ground and the load itself was laid up against the fork of a tree. It saved his putting the heavy load on the ground and the effort of picking it up again when he resumed his journey. These sticks were called *olombalachi*.

On this first trip with African carriers I had the comparative luxury of sleeping in a tent on a cot bed, but on subsequent journeys, especially in the dry season when there was no danger of rain falling during the night, I dispensed with these and slept on the ground beside a fire, along with the men. This was a most enjoyable experience. We usually made our beds in a circle, a man and a fire, alternately around a large bonfire.

Each man made his own bed. First, two heavy poles about six feet long were cut and laid on the ground about three feet apart, about the size and shape of a grave. The space between the poles was filled in with grass and leaves and the ground-sheet and blankets put on top.

After the long day's trek was over and everyone had eaten a hearty meal, the Africans' tongues were loosed. They would laugh and talk and tell stories until long past midnight. That was the time to keep a notebook and pencil on the pillow to catch new words and idioms, as well as proverbs and folklore. A favorite topic was to imitate the way the various missionaries preached and the ridiculous mistakes we made in the native language. This was all good-natured fun, and if we pre-tended to be asleep, we often heard more than we bargained for.

On our first trip to the Bangala country we started off at a bad time. The rains usually stop at the end of April, but that year they were prolonged. The first few days while we were crossing the Bié highlands the ground was dry, but when we got into the Quanza and Luandu River valleys, we found them under water. I find the following in my diary for May 13, 1925:

> "We are now in the Quanza region and much of the country is flooded. We are forced to wade with the

water at times to the thighs and waist. On crossing a swollen river by a submerged tree trunk, I missed my foothold and fell in. I removed some of my wet things and walked along in shirt and knickers until they dried. Found a human skull at the side of the path. Two and a half hours from camp brought us to the River Quanza. It is about 50 yards broad at this point. We crossed the river in a rickety dugout canoe hollowed out of the trunk of a tree. On the other side we found heavy going across a large plain about five miles wide, encountering water and mud all the way. Camped at 3:00 P.M. in an uninhabited forest after a tiring day."

Early on the journey Adcock's feet blistered and then became infected, so he had to use a hammock for a good part of the journey. This is an ordinary sailor's canvas hammock slung from a palmpole, with an awning on top to shield the person being carried from the fierce rays of the sun. Two porters carry it, but there are usually six bearers who change every half hour. They trot along much faster than the load men and sing as they go. The leader has a rattle tied to his ankle, and with this he keeps time to the rhythm of the song. The rattle is called by the Chokwes a *lusango*. This literally means "the joyful sound" and is the word which has been adapted for the gospel—*sango lipema*—the good and joyful news. The tune is well known but the words are improvised as they go along.

We were frankly disappointed at the sparseness of the population, especially on the eastern side of the Quanza. It is called "the hungry country" because of its emptiness and the difficulty of buying food of any kind. Sometimes we walked all day without seeing a single human being and then came to a little village of half a dozen grass huts with maybe 20 people. Certain areas had a group of villages gathered around a headman who called himself a "king." One such was Mwandumba, near the source of the Casai River. His name means "the lion prince." His village had about 150 people. At each of these little villages we had a meeting in the *chota* or palaver house which is a feature of every African village.

The *chota* is usually the central feature of the village. It is built in the middle of a cleared-off area and all paths lead to it. The large conical-shaped roof thatched with grass is sup-ported on poles about four feet high. The poles are spaced so that there is an opening every few feet, so that people can enter. A fire burns in the center of the earthen floor. A few low stools, made of wood and goathide, on which the elders sit, are scattered here and there. It serves the purpose of a council chamber, courthouse, and community room where tribal gossip is retailed, and where a passing stranger can spend the night, sleeping beside the fire. It is here that we usually hold our meetings.

The gospel message had a mixed reception. In some places the people were more anxious for the trader to come than the missionary, but mostly they were courteous and kind and brought small presents of manioc meal and a chicken. Our message was very simple: God is the Creator; His Son, Jesus Christ, is the Redeemer. Man is a sinner and needs to be made anew and reconciled to God. God is love and God is light. The people nod their heads and say *chamwenemwene*—"verily true!" But the impression deepens that, to get anywhere with these people, someone will have to give his life to the task, and not just half an hour's talk, like a ship passing in the night.

After nearly three weeks' walking, we reached the Kwangu River and, crossing it, entered the Bangala country. Our objective was the capital village of a paramount chief called Mwandonji. He had a great reputation and we expected great things after coming so far. A crowd of young men, with knives stuck in their belts, swaggered around boasting of the importance of Mwandonji, the great Mwandonji! All we found were a few grass huts in a low-lying plain, with no running water in the dry season. The people were practically naked and riddled with malaria. Most of the children had swollen tummies and thin spindlelegs from malnutrition and disease. A few mangy dogs roamed around among the huts. They are never fed, but they and the razor-backed pigs are the scavengers of the place.

The chief was not overenthusiastic at our presence and received us coldly. We sent him a present of twelve yards of cloth. He reciprocated by sending us a small pig and a fowl. He came to a campfire meeting at night, escorted by a body-guard of young men carrying spears. He sat on a low carved stool with a twelve-inch ceremonial dagger across his knees.

He said that three years ago Malcolm MacJannet, a missionary from Luma-Casai in Chokweland, had visited him, and promised to return and build. He said that they had all burned their idols and fetishes; but that the visitor had not kept his word, and the chief's faith in missionaries was shaken. We pointed out the difficulty of getting permission from the Portuguese to build in their country. With that remark he burst out, "Are you missionaries afraid of the Portuguese? Well, if you are, we are not!"

After seeing the Bangala country, we decided that it was an unsuitable area for a missionary center. It was low lying, malarious, with a small population, and a poor water supply. Mr. MacJannet had come to the same conclusion as we had about the unsuitability of locating in the Bangala country and later had evangelized further to the east.

Accordingly, we resumed our journey to the south. After three days we came to a place called Chitutu, where the Portuguese had built a fort with a moat. It was the border line between the Chokwe and the Songo tribes, and seemed a strategic place in relation to the surrounding country. It had elevation, plenty of water, magnificent timber forests, fertile soil, and everything to attract and sustain a good population. The Songos are a friendly, intelligent tribe and at that time were entirely unevangelized. On our journey up to this point, after we had crossed the Quanza River, we had constantly heard reports of this place. Apparently it had a reputation. Later we were to learn by bitter experience the details of its history. But for the meantime our minds were full of hope that it might make a good center for evangelization.

A Songo chief showed us a spot in the forest, with a good water supply, which would make a suitable site for building a house. The area was intersected with deep ravines covered with dense tropical undergrowth, inhabited by troops of monkeys and baboons and wild pigs. We learned later that some of these ravines had plantations of wild coffee. It was something of a mystery how the coffee had gotten there, but the most reasonable explanation was that the seed had been carried by the monkeys.

After viewing the site, we called on the Portuguese officer at the fort. He was friendly and offered to forward our application to build a house to the proper authorities at Malange, where the governor of the district lived. From there it would be sent to Luanda, the capital at the coast.

The buildings at the fort were all of mud-and-wattle construction. The officer himself was living with a black woman and appeared as if he hadn't shaved for a week. He looked pale and jaundiced, just recovering from a bout of malaria. The most prominent feature of the place was a dilapidated prison crammed with Africans, guarded by native soldiers, who stared at us in curiosity through the wooden slats in the window of the jail. After completing our negotiations with the official, we resumed our journey to the west.

After about three hours' walk, we found the body of an old man with white hair lying at the side of the path, with his head resting on one arm as if he were asleep. But on examining him, we found he was dead. As we had no means of burying him, we went on to the nearest village and reported what we had found. They told us that the old man had been held at the fort in prison as a hostage for some people who had run away. He had been kept for ten days without food, and when released had died from exhaustion and hunger on the way home. This was only a drop in the ocean of what we were to see and hear later. It was five days' walk from Chitutu back to Capango, from which we had started. The last day I walked 28 miles. This was typical of travel in those days.

As a result of this first survey of the unevangelized north of Angola, I came to a few sobering conclusions:

First, to do any lasting work would be the task of a life-time. Secondly, it would be a life of isolation. There was not much possibility that the country would be opened up to civilization in our generation. Thirdly, it would mean learning two more languages, Chokwe and Songo. The latter had not yet been committed to writing. And last but not least, it was not a job for a single man.

Subsequently I made several journeys to the Songo country with the object of following up the request we had made to the Portuguese authorities to establish a mission station at Chitutu. On one of these trips I had my first attack of malaria.

I was sleeping in a little tent in the middle of a plain on my first day out from Hualondo. A high wind blew up in the middle of the night and demolished the tent. I lay all night under the canvas, trying to hold it over the loads so that my books and belongings would not be ruined by the torrential rain which fell all night. The men were too far away to call on them for help. The next day I felt cold and ill but walked 18 miles into the mission at Chitau where Mr. and Mrs. Edwin Bodaly, Canadian missionaries from London, Ontario, were living.

A mission station is always an oasis of Christian warmth and civilization in the surrounding wilderness. Chitau was my last missionary contact before reaching the Quanza River and the unevangelized territory on the other side. A warm bath and a comfortable bed felt good, but next morning, although I was still sick and cold, I kept it to myself. It was Sunday, and Mr. Bodaly asked me to speak at the gospel service. When about halfway through with my message, my eyes would not focus and I had to stop abruptly. Mr. Bodaly helped me over to his house and took my temperature; it was 105°. I was desperately ill in Bodaly's house for six weeks. The Bodalys took care of me night and day and nursed me back to health. I owe my life to them. This was the first of many attacks of malaria. Since coming to Africa, as a precaution I had taken five grains of quinine every day, and during this attack, this was increased to twenty grains a day.

Later that year, 1926, Mr. and Mrs. Fred Olford, missionaries from Chokweland, came through Chitutu on their way to Bié. They stayed with me at Hualondo and told me that a friendly Portuguese official was in charge at Chitutu and had sent a warm invitation to me to come. He would do all in his power to obtain permission for me to open up work in the Songo country. Here was an answer to my prayers and long cherished desires from an unexpected quarter.

Chokwe Interlude

The country in which the Chokwe tribe lives lies about 300 miles to the east of Bié, where I had spent my first eighteen months in Angola. My journeys to the unevangelized north had convinced me that, in order to reach the people in that area, it would be necessary to learn the Chokwe language, which was widely spoken and understood over most of the north country. Accordingly I decided to visit the missionaries who were working among the Chokwes and get their help in learning the language.

Tom Louttit and William Maitland, from the United States, had started the work among the Chokwes in 1905. They had done the original pioneer work in the language and had opened a mission center at Boma. Later they were joined by Herbert Griffiths and Charles Aiston from England. In 1908 Mr. and Mrs. Cuthbert Taylor and Leonard Gammon opened the Luma-Casai station. In 1917 Mr. Louttit opened a third station at Buila. Cuthbert Taylor died in 1915 from blackwater fever after ten strenuous years without a break, but the work at Luma-Casai had been strengthened by the arrival of Fred Olford from England and Malcolm MacJannet from the United States.

The Chokwes are reputed to be the descendants of the Jaggas, a fierce tribe of cannibals which invaded Angola from the north in the seventeenth century. They spent their time in murder and pillage, continually drinking, dancing, and feasting on human flesh. They worshipped a huge image encircled by elephant tusks, each with a human skull stuck on its point. On the death of their chief, two wives with limbs broken but still alive were buried with him. Tribal origins are hazy and some experts discount the link of the Chokwes with the Jaggas.

The average Chokwe is a fine physical type, lean and athletically built. As with other Africans, infant mortality is high, weaklings die off in infancy. Those that live to grow up are strong and husky. A Chokwe's features are rather sharper than that of the ordinary Bantu; he does not have the flat nose and thick lips which is usual among other tribes. He has nothing of the bow-and-scrape, subservient attitude of many African natives. He has been called a "cheeky beggar," which accurately describes him.

There are only two classes in the Chokwe tribe: princes and slaves. Every boy, when he goes through the ritual in the circumcision camp, is given a new name prefixed by "Mwa". This is a title of a prince of royal blood. But Chokwe blood is all royal blood! When the first missionaries arrived in the country, no Chokwe would defile his hands with manual labor, and for many years natives of the neighboring Lwena tribe had to be imported to help with building and do the dirty work.

When I first went among them in 1925, the usual dress of a Chokwe was two antelope or monkey skins suspended from a belt around the waist, one before and one behind. He generally walked with a swagger, the skins swaying from side to side. When he sat down, the loose ends of the front skin were deftly thrown between his legs and he sat on it like a mat, while the one behind fell away like a train. Stuck in his belt, he invariably had a homemade knife, which has a thousand and one uses, from slicing barkrope to skinning an animal or carving a fetish. At the back of his head, a comb carved out of a solid piece of wood was stuck jauntily in his crinkly hair.

His ebony black face is usually tattooed; as a matter of fact, it is rare to find a Chokwe whose skin is not disfigured, either by tattooing or marks made by cupping. It is quite common to see intricate designs tattooed across the back of the shoulders, or across the abdomen, of both men and women. This is done by inserting a needle under the skin and cutting across it with a knife. Charcoal is rubbed into the wound and later the partially healed scars are rubbed with tomato leaves.

Chokwes cut their teeth into a V-shape. When Chokwes are young, and shortly after the permanent teeth appear, a block of wood is inserted in the mouth and held behind each tooth, while it is chipped down to a point with an ax or a sharp knife. When they smile, they remind one of a crocodile or a shark. A person whose teeth are not cut is taunted that he goes out at night and eats all kinds of filth, and he quickly conforms to the rule. After this treatment, the teeth soon start to decay and the missionary who possesses a set of dental forceps is kept busy.

Chokwes who are born and brought up on mission stations usually do not cut their teeth into a V-shape. But it is still a tribal custom and will cease only when the people have become completely detribalized. Children and young people who do not conform are laughed at and ridiculed. Missionaries, of course, have discouraged the custom from the beginning of missionary work.

The Chokwe headdress is an elaborate affair. The Chokwe woman makes a mixture of red earth and castor oil and plasters this on her head. It is patted down tight and gives the appearance of a skull cap with a pompadour in front. The headdress has the threefold object of adornment, protection from the sun, and keeping down the insects, of which every native has plenty. A favorite occupation in the evening, among the women and children, is sitting with one's head in another's lap, while it is being picked over for insects. A wooden pick with a little feather on the end is often stuck in the hair. This is for scratching.

As well as having the desire to learn the Chokwe language, I had another very good reason for visiting Chokweland at this time. After my journeys in the north of Angola, I had come to the conclusion that I could not live there alone. While in Portugal, I had met and seen a good deal of Elizabeth Smyth of Hartford, Connecticut, who was also interested in pioneer work in virgin territory. After her year of study in Portugal, she had gone to Luma-Casai in Chokwe-land, where she was living with Mr. and Mrs. Leonard Gammon. She and another American girl,

Kate Townsend from Buffalo, New York, had organized and were carrying on a primary school for Africans at Luma-Casai. Each morning they had to go around the houses and round up their pupils. In those days no one was anxious for education and the children wanted pay for coming to school.

Elizabeth seemed to me the ideal of a pioneer among primitive people. She had gone into missionary work of her own volition. We had common ideals and common ambitions. I decided to pay Luma-Casai a visit and venture to ask her if she would share my life among the Songo people. That meant a walk of 300 miles each way. In between lay "the hungry country." The journey from Hualondo in Bié to Luma-Casai in Chokweland occupied sixteen days. But my walk of 600 miles was rewarded! It was not an easy decision for Elizabeth to make. It meant leaving an established mission station, where there was a certain measure of comfort and orderly life, for a place where there was no civilization at all, nothing but the primeval forest and almost complete isolation. But she decided to say "yes," and I returned to Bié with my head in the clouds. We decided to get married the following year.

I wound up my affairs in Bié, bid my good friends at Chilonda and Capango good-bye, and just before Christmas 1926 made my third journey to Chokweland, again on foot. Mr. and Mrs. Fred Olford and their three children had been visiting in Bié and I joined them on their return journey to Luma-Casai. Missionaries in the Lwena country, which is another two weeks' journey beyond Chokweland in the interior, needed supplies of flour, sugar, salt, soap, and trade cloth, and we took these with us. Altogether we had a safari of about 70 men, each carrying a 60-pound load.

Before we started, each man was given two yards of cloth to buy food rations for the journey. Most of them were interior men whose only clothing was skins hanging from a belt around their waist. At the roll call, on the morning we were due to start, most of them had thrown away the skins and were wearing the white calico cloth we had given them for ration money! We pointed out to them the foolishness of attempting to cross the hungry country without rations, but they would not listen to us. The white men had their guns and plenty of ammunition and they had their bows and arrows, and game was plentiful on the plains; there would be no lack of meat although there might be a scarcity of mush to go along with it. After a lot of argument we gave up, and started our two weeks' walk into Chokweland.

Four days later the men gave up. On getting into camp, they put their loads down and said they had been carrying a 60-pound load for days without eating and they couldn't go on. With that they stalked off into the bush and left us. That evening the Olfords and I had a discussion around the campfire about what we should do. It was decided that we build a stockade with the loads and the Olfords would stay with them, while I would start back for Bié at dawn and try to recruit fresh men. Next morning at first light I started off, carrying my gun and some food for the trip.

I had been on the path only about two hours when I heard shouts behind me. A messenger had come to say that the men had come back into camp, repentant and dejected and begging our forgiveness for the way they had treated us. But they said they were starving and begged us to find some food for them. We promised to do short marches and every day to do some hunting. But for some reason the game was scarce and any animals we did see were wary and kept out of gunshot range. Every day we walked miles across the plains and only returned after dark empty-handed. One day we found the remains of an antelope which had been killed by a leopard. The men fell on it like wolves, cut it up with their knives and ate the partially decayed meat raw. They roamed the forest for edible roots and a wild fruit, called matundu, that grows beneath the ground near old village sites. But each day they became weaker and thinner.

About halfway across the hungry country, one day I was ahead of the men and saw a cloud of flies a short distance from the path. On investigating, I found the partially decomposed body of an African. Over his shoulder was a small goatskin pouch containing a letter addressed to a Portuguese trader in Bié and his hut-tax book. I found out later that the poor fellow had taken sick on his way out west, had been abandoned by his traveling companions, and had died by the roadside. When

Fred Olford came along, we dug a shallow grave alongside the body, covered him with leaves and pushed the body into the grave with two forked sticks. The frightened and superstitious carriers ran away again, abandoning their loads. We had the greatest difficulty collecting them and persuading them to continue the journey.

As we neared Chokweland, a man was relieved of his load and sent ahead to Luma-Casai to tell the missionaries of our plight. They immediately sent out several men with loads of food. We met at Cachipoke, about three days' journey from our destination. Loads were put down, fires lit, and soon the pots were boiling merrily. We stayed in camp for two days while the men did nothing but eat and sleep. It was amazing to see the transformation from weak, emaciated, disgruntled specimens of black humanity, to sleek, fat, good-natured human beings, laughing and telling stories around the fires. The last stages of the journey were done in double-quick time.

After resting up and a period of language study at Luma-Casai with Fred Olford as my teacher, I decided to take a journey up to the Songo country and build a temporary home, in the middle of the woods, to which I could bring my bride. Consequently in March 1927 I set off with 13 Chokwes on a journey of about 200 miles on foot to Chitutu. It took me ten days to get there. I took up residence in an abandoned grass hut on the side of a high hill.

The daytime was occupied in surveying the country, looking for a suitable building site with a good water supply, elevation, absence of marshes or swamps where malarial mosquitoes could breed, good timber for building and furniture making, and above all a good population among which we could work. I found what I was looking for at a spot near Quirima, by the side of a new road made by the military.

The men helped me cut down the trees and clear off the ground. We made a rectangular mark on the ground corresponding to the external walls of the house and dug an 18-inch-deep trench along the mark. Four heavy forked sticks were erected at the four corners, and beams along the top to mark the top of the walls. When this was finished, I came down with a heavy attack of malaria. I had been tramping through wet grass, being wet through again and again, and at night the mosquitoes were bad. I was sleeping in a bed bag on a heap of grass in the native hut.

One morning I awoke with a high fever and was not able to get up. I called the Chokwe headman and told him that I was sick and that he should take the men into the woods and cut hardwood logs to fill in the walls of the house, leaving spaces for doors and windows which I had marked. I was laid up for nearly a week. Each morning the cookboy came in at dawn, roused me up, and when I told him I didn't want anything, he disappeared and I didn't see him again until dark. At the end of a week the fever started to go down. I asked the cookboy to buy and cook a chicken for me. When he brought it in, I remarked that the breast was missing. It was the only part on which there was any real meat. He blandly replied that he had cut it up in such a way that there was a little piece of the breast attached to each of the other parts! The rascal had eaten it himself.

When I was able to go up to the building site, everything seemed to be going fine. The walls were up and the framing of the roof finished. A few days completed the thatching. All that remained was to cover the long walls with heavy clay, let it dry, and I would have at least four walls and a roof to which to bring my bride.

The morning after we had finished mudding the walls, I went up to take one last look at our little house in the woods. What was my horror to see that it was leaning 18 inches off the plumb on one side and nearly two feet on the other! I sent for the headman and asked him whatever had happened. He just shrugged his shoulders and said, *"kwiji"* ("who knows?"). I grabbed a heavy hoe and struck at the foundation. The hoe went right under the wall sticks. Then the headman explained that when I was sick, the men had cut a large number of sticks, but when they tried them for length, they were all too short. They thought that the simplest solution was to fill in the foundation trench with loose dirt, so that the wall stick would reach the stringer at the top. The result was, that apart from the four corner sticks, the whole house was resting on loose dirt! As soon as the heavy clay was loaded on the walls, it became top heavy, and the only thing it could do was fall over.

After I got over my shock, I told the men that I could not leave and return to Luma-Casai and tell the folks there that I had built a house, but that it had fallen down before it was completed. The men sullenly replied that I could stay if I liked, but they were going home. All but four picked up their loads and departed. But the four faithful souls who stayed worked like Trojans. We chose a fresh site and used whatever material we could from the other house. In three weeks we erected the framework of a three-roomed cottage. Local villagers helped to thatch the roof and do the final mudding.

Then we started the ten days' walk back to Luma-Casai. I had several bouts of malaria on the way and when I arrived at the mission station had to go to bed. Fortunately Dr. Laura Jacobs was there on a visit at the time. She had come from London, England, to work in Northern Rhodesia as a missionary doctor. At this time she was on a tour of the mission stations across Angola. She had discovered that most of the missionaries were suffering from hookworm. Very few of the missionary children wore shoes and most of them had it. Many of the men who had been making bricks for building, and handling the clay mud with their bare hands, had it, too. Everybody had to be examined for *ankey*, and those who had it were given the drastic treatment with carbon tetrachloride.

Dr. Jacobs undertook to get me on my feet for my wedding in June. She gave me heavy doses of quinine, but I had to stay in bed at Luma-Casai right up until the time I went to Boma to be married.

The wedding ceremony was to be in two parts. First of all, the civil ceremony at the Portuguese administration at Vila Luso. This was the legal ceremony and was to be performed in the Portuguese language by the administrator. After the civil ceremony at Vila Luso, we planned to go in Mr. Maltland's Reo Speed Wagon to Luma-Casai, about 80 miles away, and have a religious ceremony in the Chokwe language with the missionaries and the African Christians. The nearest mission station to Vila Luso was Boma, and Elizabeth had gone there ahead to comply with the two weeks' residence required in the area. I was to meet her there on the morning of the wedding.

Before leaving Luma-Casai for Boma, we were told that we would have to provide a wedding feast for the Africans. I bought a good-sized ox and Mr. Olford undertook to shoot it and divide up the meat. Unfortunately the shot did not kill it and the poor animal took off down the valley with a howling mob of Africans after it with their bows and arrows. When it finally dropped, it was like a pin cushion, with arrows sticking out of every part of its body! The carcass was cut up and carried in sizable pieces to the house, where it was distributed to the headmen for the feast. While the animal was being cut up, Mr. Olford had to stand over the crowd with a shotgun. Even so, some of the meat was slashed off with their knives and stolen. Chokwes sometimes become half crazy for meat. They have a special word in their language for meat-hunger, as they do for salt-hunger.

In view of the wedding, I had sent to Britain for suitable clothes. But they did not come in time. Dr. Barton, a man twice my size, gave me a tweed suit, and one of the missionaries, who was an amateur dressmaker, undertook to make it fit. But it was very obvious that she was not a men's tailor. The result was that the suitcoat was shaped like a bottle, with little or no shoulders. Then Mr. Griffiths, who was to be my best man, gave me a three-inch-wide linen collar. It was so large that, when I put it on, I could put my whole fist between my neck and my collar. Mrs. Gammon discovered a silk necktie in the bottom of a trunk. At the first wearing, it broke down into threads across the front. The tropics play havoc with fabrics and neckties are not much worn in the bush anyway. My outfit was completed by a pair of heavy army boots which had been used in the First World War. I had bought them from a fellow missionary.

The bride's trousseau had arrived on schedule—a beautiful white silk dress, white kid shoes, and all the accessories. She even had a bouquet of real orange blossoms from the orange trees in Mr. Maitland's garden.

Two days before the wedding, Dr. Jacobs allowed me to get up and undertake the journey to Boma by ricksha, through the bush. She gave me a letter for Elizabeth. I arrived late at night on the eve of the wedding. The missionaries had sent out a search party to look for me. On opening the doctor's letter, Elizabeth found that she had sent her warmest congratulations on our wedding, but added: "I am sorry to tell you that you are marrying this man to bury him, for he is full of malaria!" After nearly forty years, the "dying" man is still here and good Dr. Jacobs has long since gone to her reward.

Next morning early we started off in Mr. Maitland's Reo Speed Wagon for the administration office in Vila Luso. Our party consisted of Mr. and Mrs. Griffiths, Mr. and Mrs. Charlie Aiston, Mr. Maitland, the bride and groom, and some Chokwe young men.

On our arrival at the administration, the Portuguese administrator came out to meet us. He was dressed in a black cutaway coat with striped pants, white waistcoat, and patent leather shoes. He had a diamond pin in his broad cravat and was every inch the polished diplomat. But when he saw the bridegroom in his tweed suit and the army boots, I could see the shock in his face. In his confusion he nearly married the bride to the best man; he had the names all mixed up. But we got through the ceremony, which was all in the Portuguese language, somehow.

After the congratulations of the officials, we started off for Luma-Casai, where we were due to have the religious ceremony about 4:00 P.M. After this was over, we were to start on our honeymoon walk to the Songo country.

We had been on the road about an hour when we had a puncture. We all piled out and changed the tire. Ten minutes later we had another. This we had to mend. Altogether that day we had ten punctures. The tires were old and the nearest place to get new ones was the United States. The last puncture was a large rip about ten inches long. All our mending material was finished, it was eight o'clock at night, pitch dark, and we were still 25 miles from Luma-Casai. Mr. Maitland decided to take off the tire and tube and try to run on the rim of the wheel. We had been going just a few yards, when the wooden-spoked wheel went to pieces and we could go no farther.

Very dejectedly we all got out and lit a fire at the side of the road. We decided to sit by the fire all night and try to get to Luma-Casai next day. But about two in the morning we saw the headlights of a car come over the horizon. One of the wedding guests, Mr. Buchanan, a Scotch trader, who bought and sold cattle to the diamond fields, found us at the roadside and brought us into the mission station. We arrived at 4:00 A.M.

Everyone got out of bed and we had our wedding breakfast at dawn, most of the ladies in their dressing gowns and their hair in plaits. That afternoon we had the second ceremony, in the Chokwe language, in the mud-brick meeting room, performed by Mr. Louttit, the senior missionary. Mwachiavwa, the local Chokwe chief, signed his name with a cross, as one of the witnesses, on the wedding certificate. He could neither read nor write.

The sequel to the two wedding ceremonies, performed in Africa, was that several years later, when we went to England on our first furlough, we found to our dismay that the British authorities would not recognize either as legal for inheritance purposes. We had to take our two certificates to Somerset House in London, and have them registered there, to make them legal!

The missionaries were very kind in giving us wedding presents which were both useful and practical. Our old friend, Mr. Sanders in Bié, sent us twelve young grafted fruit trees: three lemon, three orange, three tangerine, and three grapefruit trees. The roots were wrapped in banana leaves and kept damp on our thirteen-day trip to the Songo country. The first thing we did on our arrival was to dig holes and plant them. After three years they started to bear. This was a great boon in a tropical land, and especially in a pioneer field where it was a problem to arrange a varied diet.

Mr. Buchanan, our trader friend, gave us two homemade chairs. They were made of heavy ironwood and each one was a man's load, but we were glad of them later on, when every piece of furniture which we needed had to be made by hand. This meant felling the trees and cutting up the lumber by hand with a ripsaw.

Immediately after the wedding ceremony at Luma-Casai, we started on our honeymoon. This involved a thirteen days' walk to the site at Chitutu in the Songo country. All our possessions had been packed in 60-pound loads and men engaged to carry them. We took along a sack of rice for food and another of rice seed for planting. We also had a bag of flour, several loads of salt for barter, and tools for lumbering, carpentry, and gardening. The first weekend was spent at a delightful spot named the Red River. As there was no need for hurry, we pitched camp each day about one or two o'clock in the afternoon, and the men went off hunting for the rest of the day. Each man carried his bow and arrows. The Chokwes are expert hunters and they never returned to camp empty-handed. Each evening we were presented with a leg of venison, with the liver and kidneys of the animal. All we could do was to cook a few slices for supper, keep some for breakfast, and give the rest back to the men. They finished every scrap each night.

After thirteen days we reached our destination. The little three-roomed mud-and-wattle house was still standing. It was at least a shelter, with four bare walls, a grass roof, and clay floor. We had a 9-foot by 6-foot tent. The men helped us to pitch it, and built a leafy bower over the top to shield it from the sun. For our bed they cut four forked sticks, stuck them in the ground inside the tent, placed logs on top for framework, then a mattress of long meadow grass, which they laced together with bamboo and barkrope. We then paid them off, and they returned to Chokweland, leaving us, a pair of innocents in the middle of the woods, among a people of whose language we did not know a single word. Fortunately there were a number of Chokwes in the area, whose language we spoke, and they were our contact with the Songo people. We slept in the tent for nearly six months, while I made doors and windows to make the little house habitable. We also cleared a piece of ground and planted a garden to raise vegetables to vary our diet.

Pioneering Under Difficulties

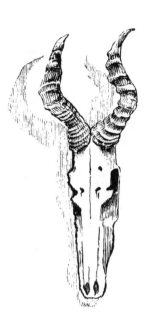

The country around Chitutu, where we were located, was heavily wooded, with thousands of beautiful hardwood trees within easy reach. There was no government restriction on cutting them. There were no softwood trees like pine or fir or larch, but there was an abundance of African teak, mahogany, and a heavy redwood called by the Africans *mushee*. The main difficulty in lumbering was that skilled labor was nonexistent. The people thought that it was beneath their dignity to work for a white man, and those that did work, would do so only for about two hours and then demand their pay. Later on, some Ovimbundu men from Bié came, and were a great help in sawing lumber, but for a long time I had to do most of it alone.

The first mistake I made was to cut down living trees full of sap. It was backbreaking work squaring the logs with an adz and sawing up the green lumber. Later I learned to choose dead trees or those that had been killed by lightning. We dug a pit, laid the squared logs across it, marked the planks with a chalk line, and ripped them up with a crosscut saw. An African boy at the bottom of the pit held one end of the saw and I the other on top. Our first efforts ended in a long wedge or two wedges with a hole in the middle. But we soon got used to it. Soon we had material for door and window frames and boards for furniture making.

The little house had gaping holes for windows and doors. Grass mats laid against them from the inside gave some privacy and kept out night prowlers. At least we thought so. We slept in the tent but had our meals in the house. We gradually acquired some chairs and a table and a couch. The latter was decorated with a couple of cushions. After a time we found that these were infested with lice and bedbugs. One night I slipped out of bed in the tent, tiptoed over to the house, pulled aside the grass mat that stopped up the door, and found an African asleep on the floor with the two cushions as pillows! He was not in the least abashed and explained that he just slipped in out of the cold, and as he had a headache, decided to use the cushions. He had never done it before and would never do it again.

One of our early problems was finding a good water supply for building. All of our water had to be carried in gourds from a deep ravine, up a steep hill, and deposited in a tin bathtub. Half a dozen wells were dug at likely spots on top of the hill but they all dried up in the dry season.

At one place I had dug a well and the water flowed in out of a hole in the sandstone. This, I thought, would be grand for drinking water and for cooking. That evening I took my wife along to see it. On approaching the spot, I saw something black bobbing up and down in the hole. When I went over to it, I found a native woman having a bath in the well. She thought it had been made to order for the purpose. It is little wonder that missionaries get dysentery or typhoid, and that every drop of drinking water has to be boiled and filtered! No water ever was thrown away. Even the bath water was used for brickmaking. To this day, I hate to see anyone turn on a faucet and allow the precious liquid to run down the drain.

Bricks were made from a mixture of red soil and anthill clay. Anthills, sometimes more than ten feet high, are found all over Central Africa. The clay in them is hard and tough. At first we built with sundried bricks, but later built kilns and burned them. When we were building our first schoolroom, I had a gang of men and boys digging the clay at the foot of an anthill, and women drawing water in gourds, which they poured into a hole in the ground. The men mixed the clay and water with their feet. The bricks were molded in a form and left in the sun to dry.

One day I sent a boy about sixteen years of age to dig at the foot of an anthill. On coming back, I found he had left the anthill and was digging a hole right in the foundation of the place we planned to put up the building. When I sent him back to the anthill, he glowered at me and said the soil there was too hard to dig. I patiently explained that we wanted the hard clay to make good bricks. On coming back, I again found him digging in the foundation. I told him that if he didn't want to do what he was told, he could go home. He had a large knife stuck in his belt. He quickly pulled it out and attacked me with it. I managed to grab his wrist and pushed it and the knife over his head, then, wrenching the knife out of his hand, I flung it into the bush. I picked up a stick and gave him a thrashing. I then made him pick up the hoe and go back to the anthill and work till quitting time. Then I gave him his pay and told him to get out, that I never wanted to see his face again. Next morning the elders of the village came in a body and thanked me for thrashing him.

"But," they said, "don't send him away; make him work and teach him to obey." I never had any more trouble with him. He later became a Christian, and many years later developed into one of the most faithful church elders we had.

We had the greatest difficulty getting work people. Every morning we had to go to the nearest village and root out the people. It was generally 9:00 o'clock before we could get started to work. About 11:00 they would come and say they were tired and ask for their pay. It was a long time before we could get any routine or any real work done. As for punctuality, that seemed impossible. The only clock they knew was the sun. They made a sundial out of a stick or straw stuck in a piece of hardened mud. No work was done in the afternoon. At first they wanted cloth for pay, but later on wanted Portuguese money to pay their government tax. When our back was turned, no work was done. They worked hard in their own fields, but to work for pay for the white man was another story.

In the early days, I don't know what we would have done without barkrope. This is the soft inner bark of certain trees, cut into strips and used in a hundred ways. It served for tying loads, securing the thatch on roofs, making mats, and was even used as clothing. This soft inner bark was beaten out with a mallet, the resultant material serving as a loincloth or blanket. I once saw a man at Chilonda, in Bié, with a complete outfit of coat, pants, and hat made of it. A corpse is often tied in it for burial. In our building work, we used literally hundreds of bundles of it for thatching and for making the mats to cover our dirt floors.

It was at this time that I had my first experience with a witch doctor. One day, after work stopped, I was counting the hoes and axes and noticed that several of the hoes were missing. Next day some more could not be found. It was evident that someone was stealing. I announced that no one would get any pay until the missing hoes were returned. We had people from two tribes working for us, Chokwes and Songos. After the pay ultimatum, they had a palaver, when the Chokwes accused the Songos and the Songos accused the Chokwes of stealing the hoes.

Finally a witch doctor was called in to settle the dispute. His method of finding the culprit was to give the poison test to a number of the leaders on both sides. Whoever was guilty would die and the innocent was supposed to vomit the poison. All this, of course, was done in the bush, without our knowledge. We had lain down for half an hour's rest after lunch, when a man rushed in breathlessly and announced that a witch doctor was giving the poison to our work people a short distance away from the house.

I ran down to the spot and found the people sitting in a circle, the Chokwes on one side and the Songos on the other. The witch doctor was in the middle with all his paraphernalia spread out on the ground. He had a goatskin bag over his shoulder, in which I surmised he had the poison (*mwaji*). I demanded that he show me what he had in the bag. He re-fused, saying that he had nothing in it but his money and his pipe. I made a grab for the bag and he gripped me round the neck with his two hands. We wrestled backwards and for-wards for a while, but he was much stronger than I, and finally I had to let him go. He gathered up his things and walked off into the forest. If I had not intervened, we would have had some dead people on our hands. This was not the end of our encounters with this particular witch doctor, but that is another story.

An item of many uses in the building was the five-gallon gasoline or kerosene can. We had, of course, no electric power of any kind. For lighting we used the old-fashioned kerosene oil lamp. Two five-gallon cans of kerosene in a wooden box was a man's load. These we could buy at railhead at Malange 200 miles away. After the oil was used, the tin cans were sterilized. They served for drawing water and storing food. They held more and lasted longer than the gourds which the Africans used.

Not only the tin cans had many uses, the wooden boxes in which they came were used for temporary furniture. Two of them set up on end, with a couple of planks on top, served as our first china cabinet. Even the nails in the lids were care-fully saved and used again. In our little dining room, two of these boxes, raised up on logs to keep them from contact with the dirt floor, on account of the termites, were covered with cretonne. On top of this was a hand-powered sewing machine.

One day I was in bed with malaria, and my wife was having her lunch alone at the table. A cat which we had brought from Luma-Casai, started hissing at something behind the box. Each time it hissed, the fangs of a snake came out, ready to strike. A native boy standing at the door, ran to get his bow and arrows. When he came back, he lifted away the sewing machine and the first box. But the snake was under the lower one, and being afraid for his bare legs, he would not touch it. However he stood poised with his bow and arrow, while Elizabeth lifted the box. Immediately the snake raised its head to strike, the arrow flew, cutting its head off clean. He used an arrow with a steel head, shaped like a crescent moon, and razor sharp. Chokwes are dead shots with the bow and arrow.

Not far from the house we were building was a Chokwe village. Sambaiyita, the headman, had formerly been a soldier in the Portuguese army during the time of the occupation of the country. At that time he had committed many crimes against his own people, for which he was thoroughly hated and feared. We did not know this at the time. He had fifteen wives and was continually sending some away and marrying others. His mother was a nice old lady. When she died, she was buried under the floor of her hut in the center of the village.

Most of our work people came from this village. Among them was a man called Somanguli. He had been accused of witchcraft in another village and had run away to Sambaiyita for protection. One day he saw me chopping a tree with a native ax. He came and took the ax out of my hand, saying, "You hold that like a woman. Let me show you how to use it!" Chokwes are blunt and forthright in what they say. Another day he found my wife planting some flowers outside the house. He asked: "What are these?" When told they were flowers to brighten up the place, he asked, "Can you eat them?" When she told him, "no," his look of pity was too eloquent for words. Somanguli's enemies finally killed him with poison.

Another man who came around every day was Siamavuloka. He wore a full beard and was distinguished looking. He had two sons working for us, who were nice boys. Day after day we were bothered by petty pilfering and one day I caught the younger boy in the act of stealing from our house. I sent for the father, told him the story, and asked him to chastise the boy, so that he would learn not to steal. He replied, "Would I beat my own flesh and blood? No sir!" They never chastise their children. When I insisted, he caught the boy by the hair of his head and hit him a blow on the back of his neck with his fist. I thought he had broken his neck. I then picked up a rod and gave him a lesson on how to do it, on the place that was meant for it. We had not been long there, when the old man came to tell me that one of his wives had run away. On inquiry I found that the "wife" was only about nine years old. It was not pleasant to find out that the people practiced child marriage as well as polygamy.

A boy from the village helped my wife with the cooking. At first we cooked on an open fire in the open air, and baked bread in a hole in the ground, lined with red-hot ashes from the fire. Later we had a wood-burning stove sent out from McClary's, the manufacturers in Canada. This was a seven-day wonder when it arrived. People would bring their friends to see the fire in the iron box, and how the smoke went up the chimney, instead of smoking us out of the house.

Whenever we sent the boy for a spoon or a knife, he would come in rubbing it between his finger and thumb, or else wiping it on his shirt. It took a long time to get any idea of cleanliness into his head, and even today it is better not to make too many inquiries or be too inquisitive behind the scenes in the kitchen. I walked in suddenly one day and found the cookboy with his fingers in a tin of condensed milk.

As well as building, at this time we planted a garden, but little realized the problems we would be up against to get anything from it. Seeds had to come from Johannesburg by mail, which meant a wait of over three months. About the only thing the Africans had for sale was small sour tomatoes. We had them so constantly that to this day I cannot bear the sight of a tomato, even the good kind. They did not have lettuce, cabbage, carrots, or cauliflower, and fresh fruit to them was unknown.

Our first problem was monkeys and baboons. The high hill on which we were building was intersected by a number of deep ravines covered with dense undergrowth, an ideal home for troops of baboons. As soon as corn was ripe, they would appear in the early morning or late afternoon. No fence could keep them out. In five minutes they could destroy weeks of work. The only way to keep them off, was to shoot at them every time they appeared. I have often seen them carry off a wounded baboon just like a team of ambulance men. Wild pigs too gave a lot of trouble. They usually operate at night. The Africans always kept guards in their fields at night, otherwise their crops would have been completely destroyed.

But our greatest enemy was the locusts. They came two years in succession. At first the Africans were delighted. There were only a few of them and they made good eating. The people pulled off the spiny legs and ate the bodies. It was an easy way of getting relish for their manioc mush. But these were only the scouts for the swarm, out on reconnaissance. When the clouds of locusts actually came, they darkened the light of the sun, in unbelievable millions. In the evening they settled on the green lush forest and fields. Every green thing was voraciously devoured; they ate even the bark of the young trees. They left death, devastation, and starvation behind. Thousands of Africans died of hunger. We tried to save as many as we could. We sent men out to Bié, six days' journey to the west, to buy food and used all the funds we had at our disposal for this purpose, but the people out there were hungry too and prices were high for any corn that was available. Many times children, who were nothing more than skeletons with the skin stretched over them, were brought to our door begging for help. Our efforts were pitifully small in comparison to the disaster.

Before the locusts left, they laid their eggs in the sand or soft earth, just below the surface. The pods of eggs were very similar to peanut shells. Neat pods of eggs, fifty or sixty at a time, bound together with a sticky, tenacious, preserving substance. Three hundred eggs or more to each female. The government did what they could to encourage the Africans to dig up these eggs and carry them to the local fort for burning. We carried literally tons of the repulsive stuff to the local administrative officer, so that they could be destroyed. The Africans say that locusts come in cycles about every thirty years and always from the north.

The Gospel Spreads
in the Diamond Mines

In 1926-1927 events had been transpiring in Bié, 200 miles to the west, which were to have widespread repercussions in another part of Angola. One evening a large party of Ovimbundu, in charge of native soldiers, passed by our house and made their camp on the other side of the hill. I was surprised to see that each man carried a New Testament and hymnbook in Umbundu. In the evening they sang and prayed around the campfires. They had come from Bailundu, in Bié, and were on their way to the newly discovered diamond fields in the Lunda district in northeast Angola. Most of them were intelligent men, of a superior type who could read and write, and nearly all were professing Christians.

They told me that a Dr. Ross, a professor of sociology from America, had visited their mission at Bailundu, and later had made a report to the League of Nations in Geneva about unsatisfactory labor conditions in Angola and how he had seen women and children being forced to work on the roads without pay or food. In reprisal an official had recruited these men by force and they were being deported to the diamond fields. The object was to smash or seriously deplete the work at Bailundu by scattering them and sending them over 800 miles away from home. That night I read with them the passages in the Acts which describe the persecution which arose after the death of Stephen, and how the scattering of the disciples resulted in the gospel spreading to other places. We had a happy time of fellowship around the fires and next day they moved on.

The history of the commencement and the development of the indigenous church work in the Lunda diamond fields is a thrilling example of how God works. The story goes back to 1913, when a prospecting engineer from the United States was treated by Mr. Maitland and Mr. Taylor when he was ill. The prospector discovered diamonds in the Lunda country and mining began some time later. During the ten years from 1921 till 1930 prayer was constantly made that the door might be opened for missionaries to enter the region with the gospel.

Reports of blessing had been filtering out, but it was not until 1931, when Mr. Maitland obtained permission from the governor of Saurimo to visit the mines, that the full extent of the work was revealed. Mr. Maitland was an amateur dentist. The governor was having trouble with his teeth and sent for Maitland to help him. While he had him in the dentist's chair, he asked the governor for permission to visit the mines, which was readily granted!

When Maitland and Louttit entered the mine area, they expected to do pioneer evangelism. Great was their surprise to find little groups of Christians coming from different directions, bringing presents of rice, meal, chickens, eggs, and even a goat. At sunrise prayer meetings idols and fetishes were burned. Some three hundred natives professed faith in Christ and thirty-three believers were baptized in one of the inlets of a crocodile-infested river. The path to the baptistry was a hippopotamus track through the reeds and grass six to ten feet high. The believers met in sheds and mud-and-wattle shacks erected by themselves. They met at sunrise for prayer and praise and reading of the Word; at sunset for a gospel service. Each place became a power center for evangelism. With this expansion came a like development of evangelistic and pastoral gift. Leaders were raised up to care for and guide the work.

As we saw that pathetic group of prisoners go off to the diamond fields in 1927, we little realized what would be the result inside of ten years. Sometimes the devil oversteps him-self.

No foreign missionary has been allowed to reside in the diamond mine area. Missionaries from Chokweland and Saurimo have been permitted to enter the territory and visit the African Christians at intervals, but the work has been completely indigenous from the commencement. It is still going on and spreading. Statistics can be dangerous and misleading, but suffice to say, the commencement and progress of the work in the Lunda diamond fields is a classic example of the historic fact that persecution often results in expansion.

More Language Study

When we arrived among the Songo people, a primary task was the learning of their language. This had never been committed to writing, but I already had a working knowledge of Portuguese, Umbundu, and Chokwe, and this was some help in making contact with the Songos and learning something of their language.

One day a man came to the door of the tent where we were living temporarily while our house was being completed. He was almost blind and nearly naked; his only cloth was a monkey skin. But he was bright and intelligent and spoke Umbundu and Chokwe and his own language was Songo. In the course of conversation it came out that for a time he had been a soldier in the Portuguese colonial army and spoke passable Portuguese. Here was our contact, ready-made, for learning Songo. He could neither read nor write and didn't know the difference between a noun and a verb, but he was friendly and a born conversationalist. He had a tiny little wife with an elaborate Songo headdress plastered with red mud and castor oil. She was like a little doll. The name of my Songo friend was Mukishi. I made a contract with him to come every day and help me to learn his language.

I had a looseleaf book lined off in four parallel columns. The first column was for a basic English vocabulary, the second for the equivalent in Umbundu, the third for Chokwe, and the last for Songo, the language we wanted to learn. Every day Mukishi would come to the tent, and later to the house, and spend an hour or so. I usually spoke to him in Umbundu and slowly and painfully worked my way through my basic vocabulary, getting about ten words each day.

In Umbundu the word for "man" is *ulume*, in Chokwe it is *lunga*, and after explaining the word in the two languages, I would ask him what it was in his Songo language. He would reply, "In our language it is *mu-ya-la, muyala*." He would tap his chest and say, "I am a *muyala*." I would write it down in the empty space in the notebook. Then we would go to the next word—"woman."

"In Umbundu it is *ukai*, in Chokwe it is *pwo*; now what is it in Songo?" He replied, "*Mu-ke-tu, muketu!*"

As time went on, and we got into deeper water, I made many silly mistakes. The golden key in learning a new unwritten language is the phrase, "What is this?" In Songo it is: "*Esi sika?*" Mukishi must have created many a laugh around the communal fire in his village as he retailed stories of the blundering efforts of the white man to learn his language. But to my face he was the soul of politeness and courtesy and painstaking patience.

After the vocabulary, of course, the grammar had to be learned and systematized. There are ten or twelve different forms of the verb, beautifully arranged, so that one can tell the exact time when an action takes place by the verbal form used.

After a time I had sufficient material to attempt a translation into Songo of the Gospel by Mark, and later the Gospel by John, with the help and check of intelligent Africans.

The various Bible Societies do an excellent work in helping missionaries in the difficult task of getting the Bible into the hands of the African people. In our early attempts at translation, we were greatly helped by word lists of the various books of the New Testament freely furnished by the American Bible Society. When I sent them the manuscript of the Gospel by John, although their experts did not know the Songo language, I was amazed by the accuracy of their criticisms. Their suggestions for improving the translation were invaluable. Dr. Eugene

Nida, their secretary for translations, has done a great work in helping many pioneer translators in this way.

The arrangement which the missionary translator has with the Bible Society is as follows: the missionary does the translation, usually with competent native help. The manuscript is sent to the Bible Society, which submits it to careful scrutiny by experts to satisfy itself that it is a faithful and competent translation of the Scriptures into the language of the people. The Society prints the books and sends them out to the missionary on the field, telling him what the books cost. The missionary sells the books to the people at a price which the people can pay. This is often well below cost. The missionary then sends the proceeds of the sales back to the Bible Society. It can readily be seen that the Bible Society is not a profit-making organization and often operates at a loss. The Society's great object is to get the Word of God, without annotation or comment, into the hands of the people, and for this reason is worthy of the practical help and support of all those who know the Lord and love the Bible.

A real difficulty in learning a language, that has not been stabilized by being committed to writing, is the fact that in a comparatively small area there may be various dialects or variations of the same language, and these are continually changing. There are as many arguments among Africans about the pronunciation of certain words as between the American, the Englishman, and the Scot. There are also differences of meaning from one district to another. A word may be used quite properly in one district, but may have an obscene meaning in another. This means that the translator must go carefully and endeavor to choose his words to suit as wide an area as possible. This is the danger of a one-man translation, or a translation by one who has not had wide experience among the people with whom he works.

It all adds up to the fact that language study is a lifetime task. New words, idioms, and phrases are constantly being learned by the foreigner. But there is no more satisfying work than to be able to give the Word of life to the people in a language which they understand. With the increase of literacy and the decreasing role of the foreign missionary in Africa, it is more and more important that the people have the Word of God in their own tongue.

Preaching the Word

When we first went to live among the Songo people in 1927, there was not a single professing Christian among them. At that time there were a number of Chokwe villages in the Chitutu area and our first friendly contacts were with them. We started with the children and the young people. The older folk were case-hardened heathen, hard drinkers, and steeped in superstition.

We taught the children Bible verses and simple choruses, which were mostly the words of Scripture adapted to a hymn tune. There was a popular song which the women used in unison when they were pounding their corn in a mortar. Words were adapted to the tune and taught to the children:

> If you hear the Words, put them in your heart;
> If you hear the Words, put them in your heart;
> If you hear the Words of Jesus,
> let your heart remember them.
> Transgression always means trouble;
> Sin always brings death!

The words and tune, both in Songo and Chokwe go with a haunting rhythm and can be easily remembered. The people are very musical and harmonize naturally and beautifully.

We had an informal service twice a day, six days a week, with people who came to work for us, and three times on Sunday for all who would come. Sometimes, after a beer drink and dance lasting all night in the moonlight, our congregation would be all drunk, and would sleep through most of the proceedings.

Instead of formal preaching, the services followed a question-and-answer pattern.

"What is your name for God?" I would ask.

"We call Him Zambi," they would answer.

"What do you know about Zambi?"

One more bold than the others would reply: "Why He created all things, the sun, moon, stars, and the earth, and He also made people."

"Do you ever pray to Zambi?"

"O, no, we never pray to Him. We pray to the spirits of our dead ancestors."

"And why don't you pray to Zambi, seeing He is the Creator and all powerful?"

Then with some hesitation: "We know that He is angry and no longer speaks to men today."

"And why is He angry?"

"Well, you see, our ancestors broke His laws and killed His messenger. Therefore He has withdrawn and we don't know anything more about Him."

Primitive Africans have folklore and traditions which are evidently corruptions of truth known to their ancestors in by-gone ages. This gives an opportunity to open the Bible and read about creation, man's fall through sin, how God sent His only Son to redeem man by dying for his sins, and the message of reconciliation to God through repentance and faith in Him. These great basic truths are explained in the simplest of language and the people interject, "*Chamwenemwene, chamwenemwene*" ("Verily true, verily true"). But it is one thing to get them to confess the truth of the message, and quite another to get them to give up their sin.

At the end of the service, when we asked them to close their eyes while we prayed to God, they flatly refused and some ran away. They thought we would do something to them while their eyes were shut.

We have often been asked what methods we used in approaching people who have never heard the message of the gospel and who have had no previous contact with missionaries. We usually tried to find out all they knew about God. Then, working from there, we tried to show them that God had revealed Himself in His works in nature, then in His Word in the Bible, and finally in His Son, our Saviour, Jesus Christ.

The pagan African is not an atheist or a polytheist. He believes in one great invisible God, the Creator and Sustainer of all things. All the Bantu languages and dialects have a name for God, but the people do not know or worship Him. They do not represent Him in any visible form. Their images and idols are representations of the spirits of people who have died.

There is a tradition that God created all things, but man has offended Him and He has withdrawn and no longer speaks to men. Therefore they have no other recourse in trouble but to the spirits of their dead ancestors, and it is to them that they pray. They make an image called a *kaponya*. When a Chokwe wishes to pray, he gets on his knees before the image, clasps his hands and says: *"Ivwa kaka"* ("Listen, my grandfather"). This is repeated several times. Then he repeats a prayer, *"Twa fwa ni Kongo, mbinga ya makwoka."* This literally means, "We died with Kongo, the horn (power) is broken."

He explains this enigmatical prayer as follows: At one time God wished to teach men, so He sent Kongo. This seems to be a heavenly being in the form of an antelope. After inquiring the way, and being directed by the sun, moon, and stars, he arrived in the upper air and was shown the way to the earth by a bird. He saw a bush path and on following it, found himself in a field where a woman was pounding corn. The woman was so excited at seeing what she thought was an antelope, that she ran to fetch her husband. He picked up the pounding stick and with one blow killed Kongo. They called the people of the village, and that night they cooked Kongo and had a feast.

After a time God came to look for Kongo, for He knew that he was dead. He first accused the sun, but the sun protested his innocence, and to prove it, said he would rise the next morning. He rose as usual and so was absolved. The same happened with the moon and the stars, and they too were cleared of guilt in the death of Kongo. Finally God came to man and accused him. But he denied all knowledge of the death of Kongo, so God said, "I will kill you, and if you are innocent, you will immediately come to life again." With that God struck him dead, and the people gathered around to see what would happen. As the days passed by, a decomposing corpse was proof to everybody that the man was guilty of the death of the teacher whom God had sent. Since then God has withdrawn from man and left him to his own devices. (The Songo people have a slightly different version of the story, but it is substantially the same.)

After making his prayer of confession about the death of Kongo, the pagan Chokwe or Songo then prays for what he wants. He believes that the spirit represented by the image hears his prayer and is able to answer by causing either good or evil. Actually it is a form of spiritism or demon worship.

Very many of the beliefs and traditions of the Bantu people seem to show a corruption of early light which they had in the dim distant past. There is little doubt that, sometime in their history, their ancestors had contact with Semitic people. For instance, their language has certain verbals and idiomatic forms which have an affinity with the Hebrew language. Then there is the rite of circumcision which is very widely practiced. An uncircumcised man would be ostracized or even cut off from the tribe. The poison ordeal seems to be a corruption of the jealousy test of Numbers 5:11-31. In certain cases, after the death of her husband, a woman goes through a purification ritual, which is identical with baptism by immersion and has a similar meaning. They have a corrupted version of the tower of Babel.

All this goes to show the truth of the description of the pagan world in Romans 1:19-32: *"Because that which may be known of God is manifest in them; for God hath shewed it unto them...Because that, when they knew God, they glorified Him not as God...and changed the glory of the uncorruptible God into an image made like to corruptible man, and to birds, and fourfooted beasts, and creeping things. Wherefore God...gave them up to uncleanness."*

This was the background in which we had to commence our work. Polygamy, child marriage, witchcraft, fear, superstition, drunkenness, drumming in the night, dancing in the moonlight, and the hopeless and bloodcurdling death wail when someone was dying. This was the environment in which we lived.

At first we had no meeting room and the people were afraid to come, anyway. We held our services for the work people in the shade under the trees. Two useful methods for breaking down prejudice were a school for the young people and the treatment of the people when they were sick. Both started in a very simple and elementary way, but later were organized and developed.

One day an old lady came and holding up her hand, said, "*Ngana*, could you help me?" One of the fingers had been injured and was decomposed, with the bone exposed up to the second joint. There was no alternative but to amputate it. I went into the tent and asked my wife,- who had had a year's nursing experience in a maternity hospital, in preparation for the mission field, if she would like to undertake it, but she declined. We had no surgical instruments or anaesthetics of any kind. The nearest doctor was over 200 miles away and, if you wanted to get there, you had to walk! I sterilized a razor blade; the poor old soul put out her hand and turned her head away. She never flinched or made a sound while I severed the finger at the joint and made a little flap of healthy skin and flesh and folded it over the top and bound it up. It healed very nicely and she and her family became our fast friends.

We of course were very much opposed to the African system of child marriage and to certain secret societies, where children of both sexes at an impressionable age were instructed in immoral practices when they were initiated. To counter our disapproval, the elders told the children gruesome stories about us, such as, that we had cut off a native's head and hid it under the place where we preached, and that we made a practice of extracting black children's eyes with which to make eye medicine. The result was then, when we went into a Songo village, the children would run helter skelter, and all we could see was a bevy of black legs disappearing into the grass.

The first publicly to confess Christ as her Saviour was a Chokwe cripple girl called Mahako. As a child she had been sold as a slave in the far interior. The mother had died on the way out to Bié, and the child had been pushed into a long narrow basket and carried on top of a load. As a result she had crooked, deformed legs and was a hunchback. She came regularly to our meetings, learned the choruses, and drank in the Word. The love of God, in sending Jesus to die for her sin, touched her heart. When she told the village elders that she had decided to become a Christian, they beat her with a whip and threatened to take her life. But her bold stand was an encouragement to others, with the result that many of the younger folks came to the school and the meetings, and be-came Christians, too.

Mahako's life and even her personal appearance was completely changed. On account of cruel treatment received as a child, she had a hard face and a sarcastic bitter tongue; but the grace of God altered all that. Later she married a man called Kapiha, who also had been a slave and whose life also had been changed by the gospel. He was a herdsman, who on several occasions risked his life by defending the cattle against lions, with nothing more than a spear. He was later conscripted and sent to the diamond fields on forced contract labor, and was there killed by a foreman striking him with a hammer; so Mahako was left a widow.

While our house was being built at Chitutu, a fine-looking African of the Chokwe tribe came and asked for a job. His name was Chiteta. His wife, Chambishi, came with him and they built a grass hut near us. He was an expert thatcher and he helped cover our roof with fine meadow grass. Day after day he came to the gospel services, which were held twice daily, at 6:00 A.M. and 7:00 P.M. Soon it was very evident that he was troubled about his past life, and after a while he came to tell us that he wanted to be a Christian.

It was the custom that anyone who wished to renounce his pagan past, and accept Christ as Saviour and Lord, would stand up publicly in a meeting and say so before their fellows. Both Chiteta and his wife did this about the same time.

Chiteta had had some training as a witch doctor and had been in the habit of telling fortunes for a living. A short time after his conversion, one of his legs suddenly swelled up without any apparent reason, and also a piece of bone came out of his child's hand. To an African, these are unmistakable signs of witchcraft.

He then came and told us that he still had some fetishes in

his hut, which were troubling him, and he used the proverb often quoted by Chokwes, "Throw away the honeycomb and the bees will leave you." The honeycomb to him was the accouterments of his old trade of fortunetelling, and the bees were his old colleagues in witchcraft. Next Sunday he brought the filthy bundle to the meeting, and we publicly consigned them to the flames. As they went up in smoke we sang, "My chains are snapt, the bonds of sin are broken, and I am free." Some of the older folks kept at a respectable distance, as they were afraid that something dreadful would happen.

A short time afterward I left on a journey to the other side of the Songo country. While I was away, Chiteta took sick, as did his children. Finally some men came and carried him to his home village. On my return I found he had gone. News filtered in from time to time of his illness and finally a runner came to say that he had died.

Next morning I set off with three Africans and walked about 24 miles to his village. On arrival we found a number of old men sitting in the palaver house. They refused to help us in any way and pointed to the grass hut where Chiteta had lain unburied since his death several days previously. We found his naked and mutilated body in a hut devoid of furniture of any description. He had been poisoned and was lying on the bare ground.

We had no means of making a coffin, so we went outside and asked the men of the village, who were making grass and bamboo doors for their huts, if they would let us have some bamboo and barkrope to make a basket in which to bury him. This they refused to do. I finally persuaded some little boys to cut some, while the Christian young men who had come with me dug a grave in the bush. Not one of the villagers would touch the body, so we had to wrap him up ourselves, tie the bundle to a pole and carry him to his last resting place in the forest. I asked the headman to come with me to the grave.

"No!" he said. "The dead man followed the teaching of the white man and this is what has come of it." After repeated invitations and argument, some of the men and boys came with me to the burial. Some were afraid to come near, but peeped from behind trees while I preached to them over the open grave.

Chiteta lost his life because he threw away his honeycomb and made a complete break with the old pagan life.

Chiteta's wife, Chambishi was the pledge for an unredeemed debt, and when her husband died she was taken several days' journey away and married to a heathen cripple. She of course was not consulted in the matter. She was blamed by the village elders for killing her husband. She had a little girl about four years old, and one evening she took the child with her, while she went looking for mushrooms for her evening meal. She left the child by an anthill while she was foraging around, but when she came back the child was gone. A search was made but she could not be found.

Next morning the mother set off to look in the surrounding villages and found her in a little hamlet across a large river, much too deep and broad for her to cross alone. On reaching home with the child, Chambishi went to prepare some food, but before she got it ready, the little girl dropped dead. It was another case of poisoning. Several other members of the family died under mysterious circumstances. The news spread far and wide that it was a dangerous thing to insult the spirits of their ancestors and become a Christian.

One day, early in 1929, the Portuguese officer in charge of the local fort suddenly appeared with a number of native soldiers. He told me that he had heard that a man and his wife had been killed near our house. He had come to investigate. One of our workmen called Sambonge was standing nearby. The officer ordered him to be tied and beaten.

We had been warned again and again by the authorities that we must never interfere with the military or the officials in the execution of their duties! If we did we could be turned out of the country.

The soldiers tied Sambonge's wrists together, made him bend over and then lashed his bare back with a hippohide bull whip. Each blow lifted a weal of skin about three inches long. I watched until I was sick and then protested to the officer that the man had been working for me and that, as far as I knew, he had nothing to do with the killing.

"Well," he replied, "on your recommendation I will let him

go, but this is the only way to extract information from these people!" Sambonge seemed to have aged about twenty years in five minutes. He crawled off to his village with the blood dripping down his back.

I then guided the officer to the nearest Songo village over the crest of the hill. We found a number of old men sitting around. These were arrested and bound by the soldiers. Each man had his hands tied behind his back and each one was tied to the other with a rope around his waist. The officer threatened the headman with a gun, and he, trembling from head to foot, consented to take us to the place where the crime had been committed. We set off single file through the forest behind the Africans, the headman leading the way, with a soldier pointing a gun at his head.

In a few minutes we came to a clearing about a mile from our house. There were two heaps of dry sticks, one at each side of the clearing. The headman was untied and ordered to remove the sticks. After some hesitation and a few blows with the hippohide whip, he complied. When the sticks were removed, we saw two tunnels going into the ground, where wild pigs had been burrowing, and out of each one protruded two human feet. A man called Chambasuku and his wife had been killed by the poison ordeal to settle a trivial question of land rights, and their bodies had been pushed head first into the burrows and covered with firewood, which later would be set alight.

The two men responsible for the deaths, Sakenda and his brother, were arrested and taken to the fort. For some obscure reason, which I could never understand, Sakenda, who was the witch doctor, was later freed, but the brother was sent to Fort Roçadas in the south of Angola, where he died.

This case seemed to be a crisis at the commencement of our work. A number of boys who were present at the terrible proceedings that day later came to us. The men arrested and deported were ringleaders in opposition to our work. With its leaders gone, the village broke up. Most of the boys and young men were sent away to forced labor at the sugar plantations at the coast, but after two years they returned.

Among them were Kasenze and Mwaku. Both soon made a

profession of faith in Christ. Kasenze especially was a bright case; he made steady progress from the start, soon learned to read, developed into a good gospel preacher and expositor, and was a great help in translation work in the Songo language. His mother and other members of the family became believers. Many years before, his sister had been stolen by Biheans, when she was a child, and sold into slavery. By a strange chain of circumstances, they found out where she was, and brought her back, so that she could hear the gospel. She too professed faith in Christ. Kasenze later went to a center in the Songo tribe, called Wassunga, and built up a prosperous work. He was a hard worker, a gifted linguist, and a leader in every sense of the word. Sad to say he was executed by Portuguese soldiers at Nova Gaia in the troublous days of March 1961.

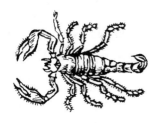

Blackwater Fever

After two years of work, our little mud-and-wattle home in the woods was finished and furnished with homemade furniture, all handmade. A crude meeting room had been built, school and medical work organized, as well as regular meetings for preaching and teaching. A number of Chokwes had confessed Christ as Saviour, had been baptized, and the foundations of a New Testament Church laid.

During this time the Lord had given us our first child, a little boy. For the birth we decided to go down to Luma-Casai, where we had been married. This meant a ten days' walk in the wet season. Elizabeth had a hammock and bearers to help her over the hard places. The worst experience was crossing the Kuhafu River, which was in flood. All the stick bridges had been carried away by the current. We camped on the river bank, while I went up and down the river, looking for a ford where we could cross without having to swim. I found a place where the water was up to the shoulders of the men at its deepest point. The African carriers suggested that Elizabeth lie down on the wooden framework of the awning of the hammock; then two men hoisted this on top of their heads, and with two other men balancing the burden on either side, they walked across the river, with the water often up to their necks.

When we arrived at Luma-Casai, we found our old friend Dr. Jacobs was there as well as Susan MacRae, a very competent nurse from Framingham, Massachusetts. Our first child, David, was born on April 1, 1928, in the home of Miss MacRae. There were complications and we were very thankful for the skill and care of the doctor and nurse who saved Elizabeth's life. If it had not been for their devoted help, she would have died. When the baby was a few weeks old, we returned to our home at Chitutu.

The Lord later gave us two other children, Thomas Ernest in 1932, and Elizabeth Ann in 1935. While our children were growing up, we did not have a doctor or registered nurse within reach, and although they were exposed to all kinds of tropical disease and accident, we are thankful that they were preserved from serious illness and grew up strong and healthy.

When baby David was nine months old, Elizabeth came down with blackwater fever. We had made several itinerating journeys in the Luandu River region where there are a lot of swamps and Anopheles mosquitoes. Both Elizabeth and I had been having recurrent attacks of malaria and in her case it ended in blackwater fever. This is a most serious and often fatal disease. The blood cells break down and are passed in the urine, which turns a dark brown, coffee color, which gives the disease its name. Many of the early missionaries died as a result of this malady.

When this occurred it was the month of November, in the middle of the wet season. We were alone in the depths of the woods, our nearest neighbors being the Bodalys at Chitau in Bié, six days' journey to the west. I wrote a letter to Mr. Bodaly, telling him what had happened, hoping that someone might be able to come to our help. I gave the letter to a Chokwe, called Mwachingongo, gave him a storm lantern so that he could travel after dark, and told him to get out to Chitau as quickly as he could. He could have done the journey in four days, traveling without a load, but, instead of hurrying, he loitered along the way and took about a week to get there. He told me afterwards that he thought the *Ndona* was going to die anyway and there was no use in hurrying!

In the meantime, I handed the baby over to a native girl to care for him, and I gave all my time and attention to Elizabeth.

There was, of course, no medical help of any kind available, and while there was a government post about five miles away, the Portuguese officer in charge was absent, and in those days there was no radio communication or telephone contact with the outside. At that time I had never seen a case of blackwater, although we have taken care of many since. For over a week I did not go to bed, but dozed and catnapped in a chair when I could. On the ninth day, Elizabeth had a relapse and I thought the end had come. On the thirteenth day she had a second relapse with uncontrollable hiccoughs, and again I gave up hope.

One day I heard what sounded like the hoot of an automobile horn, but thought I must have been dreaming and paid no attention. But then it sounded again. I went to the door and found two white men standing on the porch with the rain dripping out of their clothes and a little automobile outside. It was Mr. Bodaly with his fellow worker, Edwin Roberts, an Englishman from London.

They had made an epochal journey from Chitau in the little auto under the most difficult conditions. There were two large rivers to cross, the Quanza and the Luandu, without bridges. Between the two rivers there was practically no road at all. The military, years before, had hacked a road through the virgin bush, but it was overgrown and covered with anthills and good-sized trees. When they came to the first river, the little car, an early compact called a Jowett, was lifted into two large dugout canoes, the two side wheels in each canoe tied together, and then paddled across. In the overgrown bush, an African rode on the running board, with an ax to chop down the trees which blocked the way. Again and again they had to be pushed and lifted out of swamps.

Their arrival was an indescribable relief and encouragement. Edwin Roberts was a comic. He described their incredible journey across the swamps in such a funny way that we laughed until our sides were sore. All our anxiety and troubles were forgotten.

Mr. Bodaly then told us that he must get back home the next day. But when we looked in the gas tank of the car it was nearly empty and the oil level was dangerously low. Needless to say there were no gas stations in the vicinity! But I had a good supply of kerosene which we burned in our lamps, and we filled up the tank with this. The Songo women had the custom of putting red mud and castor oil on their heads, so crude castor oil was easy to obtain. We filled up the sump of the car with this. Next morning Mr. Bodaly had some difficulty getting the little auto to start, but finally he got it going. As far as I know he has never told the story of his return journey to Bié, burning kerosene and crude castor oil in the car, but he finally made it. Unfortunately it was the last journey that the long-suffering auto ever made! But we are most grateful to our good missionary friends and to the little car that gave its life to bring us help and comfort, and without a doubt saved my wife's life.

Mr. Roberts stayed with us and, after Mr. Bodaly had left, we had a serious talk about what we should do. Roberts had had considerable experience in medical work. He told us quite frankly that Elizabeth would not recover if we stayed where we were. We must get her out to Bié and send for competent medical help.

"But," I exclaimed, "how can we get her out in the middle of the wet season, in the rain, and across the flooded country between the Quanza and the Luandu Rivers?" Blackwater patients must lie flat on their back; if they attempt to sit up, there would be a relapse.

"Well, let's pray about it," he replied. We asked God, if it was His will that we get out to Bié, that He would stop the rain for about a week until we arrived there. This seemed presumption when we considered the time of the year and the heavy rains which continued day after day. But we were up against it and had no alternative.

We sent for the local chief and told him what we planned to do. He promised to have men at the door the next morning to carry the hammock and the loads. When we awoke at dawn the rain had stopped, so we decided to start. A sailor's hammock slung from a palmpole, with a canvas awning over the top and sides, was prepared to carry the patient, and a smaller one to carry the baby. We put him in a basket, which was secured in the hammock with straps. Bed loads, food boxes, a tent in which to sleep at night, and odds and ends for the journey were hurriedly prepared and tied up.

The native porters carried the hammock into the bed-room, we wrapped Elizabeth in the blankets on the bed and carried her out. I quickly tidied up the place, turned the key in the door, and followed the men, the hammocks on ahead, the loadmen in single file, and Roberts and I bringing up the rear on foot. That day we pushed on until sundown. We covered over 30 miles and no rain had fallen. When we reached camp, we opened up a folding cot bed, lifted Elizabeth out of the hammock, and carried her into the tent. That night we had a praise meeting around the campfire. The Lord had answered our prayer for one day.

Next morning we were up early and on the path shortly after dawn. In the afternoon we ran into our first serious problem. The Luandu River, swollen with the heavy rains, was about 100 yards broad and a swift current was tearing at its banks. The river too had both hippos and crocodiles. The only means of crossing was a frail dugout canoe which, when loaded with the paddler and a man with his load, was just about three or four inches above the surface of the water. When I looked at it my heart sank. But the paddler assured us that he could take the hammock with its burden safely across. He told us to fill the canoe half full of leaves, lay the hammock and patient on top and leave the rest to him! I went up to the hammock, explained the situation to Elizabeth, and asked her what she thought about it. If she was nervous and would rather not attempt it, we would turn back to our home at Chitutu. She said she would rather go on, she would keep her eyes shut, and for us to get on with the job.

We carried the hammock down the bank, laid it in the bottom of the canoe, but held our breath when the paddler stepped in. The Songo paddlers stand up in the canoe and balance it with their two feet and the weight of their body. He did a magnificent job, paddling along the bank against the current upstream, then gently nosed the canoe diagonally with the current across the river and made a perfect landfall at the crossing. In the meantime I had stayed on the bank with a loaded and cocked gun, in case a croc or hippo should show its head. The hammock on the other side was lifted out and slung in the forks of two trees, while men and loads were ferried across. For the second day no rain had fallen, and we had another prayer and praise meeting that night around the campfire.

Our last hurdle was the Quanza, a much larger river than the Luandu, but with much more sturdy dugouts for the crossing. A Portuguese trader called Sobral came down to the river with two Songo natives, who he said would take the hammock across. Instead of laying it in the bottom of the canoe, they proposed to stand up, with the ends of the palm-pole on their shoulders, and the hammock swinging in mid-air. This seemed a nerve-racking experience for the patient, and again I asked her what she felt about it, and got the same reply as at the Luandu, "Let's get on with it." Men and loads were again safely transported to the other side.

Here Mr. Bodaly met us with a truck and soon we were at his home at Chitau. A guest room had been prepared with a comfortable bed and white sheets, which to us looked like a palace. We carried the patient in and then I went out to pay off the men.

They were lined up on the verandah. While we were standing there talking, the great dark thunder clouds were gathering overhead, and before we had finished settling with the carriers, it had started to rain. We had been on the path for five days and not a drop of rain had fallen during the journey. Roberts and I looked at each other, but we couldn't speak. All we could think of was the little prayer meeting in the mud-and-wattle house at Chitutu when, in simple faith, we had asked the Lord to stop the rain until we got out to Bié. He had done just that! That year we heard of four other cases of blackwater fever among white people in Angola. All four died; Elizabeth was the only one who recovered!

Again at Chitau we received much kindness and gracious hospitality from the Bodalys and the Roberts. Dr. Jacobs was visiting in the vicinity, and as soon as she heard of Elizabeth's illness, she hurried over and undertook to nurse her back to health. But as soon as Elizabeth could walk, the doctor told us that we must go home on furlough for a complete rest and change. So at the end of 1929 we left Africa for Britain and America. The few African believers left at Chitutu had to carry on alone, until our return to Angola in 1930.

While in London, England, we had an interview with Sir Phillip Manson-Bahr, a specialist in tropical disease. He gave us some expert advice on how to take care of our health and avoid a recurrence of the dread blackwater fever. We are thankful that, although we were exposed to the same conditions for many years, we never had another attack.

In 1931 the work was given a fresh impetus by the arrival of David B. Long, from Belfast, Ireland, and a year later by his fiancee, Eleanor Archibald, from Truro, Nova Scotia. David, who already spoke fluent Portuguese, quickly mastered both the Chokwe and Songo languages. The Longs did a most valuable work during the five years they were with us. After their first furlough in Canada, where they were held up for a time by the outbreak of World War II, they settled at Luma-Casai in Chokweland, where he has done an expert job in the revision and translation of the Bible in the Chokwe language. The translation of the Old Testament was completed by David Long in June 1967. Thus the Chokwe people now have the whole Bible in their language.

Journeys on Foot

The first baptism at Chitutu took place early in 1929, before our furlough. Three Chokwe young men, the firstfruits of our work, were baptized by Malcolm MacJannet, of Chokweland, who was paying us a visit at the time. Immediately after the baptism we had our first meeting for the observance of the Lord's Supper, when seven of us, three Africans and four whites, sat down in communion to remember the Lord in His death, as directed in 1 Corinthians 11:24-26. Our meeting room was an open shed with a grass roof and dirt floor, the seats were roughhewn logs, but the Lord's presence was very real and very precious.

We were able to buy wine for the service from a Portuguese trader about five miles away. From the beginning we tried to keep everything as simple as possible, and not initiate anything which the Africans could not do themselves without our presence. The bread was often baked in a hole in the ground lined with red-hot ashes, or in a Dutch oven made of clay and shaped like a beehive. From the start, both the Chokwe and Songo languages were used in the meetings, with occasionally a hymn in Portuguese. As the people became more familiar with the Portuguese language, it was increasingly used, both in school and in preaching. The use of English, of course, was prohibited entirely by law.

Most of the early converts were Chokwes, but as time went on we were able to win the confidence of the Songo people. One of the first Songos to profess faith in Christ was Sakaya. He had been a slave and, after his release, had come to me for work. The only job I could offer him was to cut grass for thatching. He came to the early morning and evening meetings, where the narratives and parables of the Saviour concerning the way of salvation were simply and systematically explained.

The message was plain and to the point: Man is a sinner and a rebel against God. He is in danger of eternal banishment from God on account of his sin. He needs to repent and turn to God. But God loves sinners; He sent His Son, Jesus Christ, to reconcile man to Himself. He, who was sinless, died as a substitute for sinful man on the cross. God, to show His approval and satisfaction with the death of His Son, raised Him from the dead on the third day. His precious blood, shed for us, can take our sins away. We must repent, abandon our sins, and trust and follow Him as our Saviour and Lord. These truths were hammered home day after day. We must have a new life and a new power, be "born again," if we want to see and have communion with God.

After one of these meetings, Sakaya stood up and said that he wished publicly to confess Christ as his Saviour and Lord. Then he asked me for a copy of the Scriptures. At the time I had only a few precious copies of the New Testament in Chokwe and Portuguese, which were not languages which Sakaya spoke. I reminded him that he was not able to read and that I was reserving the books for those that were able to use them.

"Sell me the book," he replied, "and I will learn to read it!" Again I had to tell him that the books were so scarce and precious that I must keep them for those that were able to read. He went away very crestfallen.

A few days later he came back and asked me if I had a load he could carry from railhead. I told him I had a load of window glass at Coemba, about 200 miles away, which he could bring and I also had another load which I wished to send to Monte Esperança, which was near Coemba. Next day he came, with a little boy carrying his bundle of food; he picked up his 60-

pound load and started on his 400-mile journey. He was away about a month.

The day he arrived back with the heavy load of glass, and letters from fellow missionaries, I greeted him in the usual native fashion, when we exchanged the gossip of all that had happened since he had been away, and he told me of his experiences along the path. I then invited him to the house to give him his pay. I asked if he would like money to pay his tax to the government or cloth for his wife. He looked at me for a moment with a quizzical expression on his face.

"Would you really give me what I want for my pay?" he asked.

"Certainly, whatever you want," I answered. "Is it money or cloth?"

"What about that New Testament?" he replied.

Suffice to say, Sakaya got the book and his pay as well! He went off, holding the precious copy of the Word to his breast, and patting it as he went up the path to his hut. In a short time, using the New Testament as a textbook, he learned to read, and became a very effective leader and preacher among his own people. He was most intelligent. He could stand up with a Chokwe New Testament in his hand, and translate it into his own Songo language without a pause, and then preach in Songo. He also became fluent in Chokwe and could speak passable Portuguese.

Sakaya earned his living by sawing boards, work he learned after he became a Christian. He married a fine Songo girl but for a number of years they had no children. Then, in answer to many prayers, Samuel was born. He was the apple of their eye. When he grew up, he went to school and later became the school teacher in the village where his father had become the headman.

In the troubled days at the beginning of 1962, when military forces from Portugal were dashing about the Songo country, Samuel became frightened and ran away. A jeep stopped at Sakaya's village. The officer in charge asked for the headman. Sakaya was questioned and when the soldiers found that his son had fled, they took Sakaya out and shot him. As far as we know he was not guilty of any crime, but was a simple evangelical believer who had always been loyal and respectful to the government authorities.

One of the most extraordinary journeys, that I have known, was undertaken by a crippled African called Sawuchika. I first met him in a Chokwe village on the Kuhafu River, near the source of the Kwangu. I was traveling from Luma-Casai to Chitutu with native carriers, and one evening, as the sun was going down, I reached this village. After preparing our camp for the night and having something to eat, I went down to the village, as our custom was, for a meeting. A good crowd gathered in the little palaver house around an open fire, and I had an enjoyable time telling them from John 3:16 about the love of God in sending His Son to redeem fallen man. A circle of seminude Africans squatted on the ground around my feet. When I had finished, the headman interjected with a question:

"Where does the sun go at night?" he asked. "Does it go into a hole in the earth, or into a hole in the water?"

I tried to give him a simple lesson on astronomy, illustrated by two fruits about the size of an orange and a plum, representing the sun and the earth. I patiently explained that the earth was a globe revolving on its axis, and at the same time describing its orbit round the sun. The side facing the sun was in daylight and the side away from the sun was in darkness, making the day and the night.

"Is that what you believe," he exclaimed, "that we are standing on a ball, moving in two ways at the same time? Why, the white man must be crazy to believe anything so ridiculous as that!"

I felt rather weary and discouraged. We had walked more than 20 miles that day and although we would rather have lain down in our sleeping bags and gone to sleep, we had come down to the village to preach the gospel, and it had ended in a ridiculous argument about where the sun goes at night!

The fire had died down, but suddenly, in the darkness outside, I saw an object creeping along the ground on all fours. It looked like an animal on the prowl. I instinctively reached for my rifle, which was resting against the supporting sticks of the palaver house, loaded and cocked it, for, in the dark, the creature looked like a leopard or a hyena. The men started to laugh, however, and as the object approached, I saw it was a human being, crawling on his hands and knees. He came in and squatted beside the little group.

"Who are you?" I asked.

"My name is Sawuchika," he replied. The name means "The father of abandonment."

"How did you get your name?" I asked.

"I used to be a man like another man," he said. "I could walk and work and hunt. But one day I came down with a high fever, I had pain in my head and back and legs and I thought I was going to die. The elders sold my wife and two boys into slavery, thinking I wouldn't get better. If an old woman hadn't taken pity on me, and brought me some food and water occasionally, I would have died of starvation. When I did recover, my legs were withered and I could only crawl on my hands and knees like this. Now I am Sawuchika, the father of abandonment."

Apparently his sickness had been polio. When I looked at him in the semidarkness, I could see a magnificent, intelligent head, broad shoulders tapering down to a thin athlete's waist, but his legs were just the bones with skin draped over them. His knees had calluses like a camel and the knuckles of his hands, too, were swollen and callused from dragging himself around.

I repeated to him the text of the evening: *For God so loved the world, that He gave His only begotten Son, that whosoever believeth in Him should not perish, but have everlasting life.* He looked at me in wonder and said, "I never heard that before. I thought nobody loved me." I explained the verse to him, sentence by sentence.

"Thank you," he said abruptly, and gave me the Chokwe farewell, "*Sala kanawa*" ("Remain well"), and crawled out into the dark.

After bidding the people goodnight, I went up to the campsite and laid down beside the fires, along with the men. Next morning we were off before dawn on our long trek to Chitutu, about 120 miles further on.

About a year later, one day on coming out of the house, I saw something dark coming through the grass on the edge of the clearing, some distance away. We had been having trouble with baboons raiding the garden, and I went into the house to get my gun. But on coming out, I saw it was a human being, painfully crawling on his hands and knees across the clearing. When he reached me, he sat on the ground, clapped his hands, and gave me the Chokwe greeting: "*Moyo, moyo!*" I recognized him immediately as the man I had seen in the little hut at the Kuhafu 120 miles away.

"Surely you're not Sawuchika?" I said.

"Yes," he said, "I am. I'm glad you haven't forgotten my name."

"How did you get here?" I asked in astonishment.

"I came the way you see me, on my hands and knees."

"How long did it take you to come?" I asked.

"Oh, about nine moons (months)," was his reply.

"But you couldn't have been crawling like this for all that time, surely?"

"Well no, not exactly. After a week or two on the path, my knees and knuckles broke down into sores and they bled, so I had to rest until they healed. This happened four or five times, but I kept on going when they got better."

"And how did you feed yourself on the path?" I asked.

"Well, you know, *Ngana*, the people in the villages are good in giving me food, and then, although I cannot stand up, I am a good hunter and I have my bow and arrows. I stalked and shot *kai* (deer) as I came along, and exchanged the meat for corn and sweet potatoes in the villages."

When I got over my surprise at his story, I asked, "Sawuchika, whatever brought you all this long journey?" He was silent for a moment.

"I can never forget the story you told me that night beside the fire at Maha Chilemba," he said. "I thought that nobody loved me, the father of abandonment. That word was like an arrow in my heart. I got no rest until I made my decision that I would have to hear it again. I want to stay here so that I can hear it every day."

Sawuchika later told us that, when he first heard the Word, it was like an arrow in his heart, but now he had found the healing balm. He publicly confessed his faith in the Saviour and was baptized as a believer. I made him crutches and tried to teach him to use them. But his muscles were so sore, after trying to walk upright, that he decided to discard the crutches and continue to crawl on his hands and knees. We never found his wife, but, through the help of a Portuguese official, were able to locate his two boys. Unfortunately one of them had contracted leprosy. The last time I saw Sawuchika was at a little outpost called Sautar, where there is a group of African Christians. The recent tide of trouble and bloodshed has swept over that place, too, and all we can do is to pray that God will preserve His own.

The longest walk I ever accomplished without a night's rest was about 110 miles. The Portuguese administrator had sent for me to transact some official business at Nova Gaia, where he lived. The only means of transport I had in those days was a bicycle which had seen better days. I arrived there without incident and finished my business. But in the middle of the night a messenger arrived with some disturbing news that meant I had to get home in a hurry. A few miles out the bicycle broke down and I left it with a man in a hut at the roadside, and started to walk.

It rained during the night, and I stumbled and slid along in the red gumbo soil, which was over an inch thick on the soles of my shoes. I walked the rest of the night and all the next day. As the sun was going in, I came to a river called the Jombo, where I found some of my men. They invited me to spend the night with them in a grass hut on the bank of the river. But I told them of my anxiety to get home and asked for a volunteer to come with me. A young Chokwe, called Thomase, picked up his ax and said, "*Tatuyenu*" ("Let's go").

It was dark as we started and there was no moon. He went ahead and I followed, holding on to his belt. After some hours, he suddenly wrenched himself free from me and ran on ahead.

"*Achi chika*?" ("What is it?") I shouted at him.

"It was a leopard eating an antelope, but I have chased it away. Come on!" he shouted back.

Sometime in the middle of the night I saw a light come up over the horizon. It was so bright, I thought it must be a flashlight in the distance, but it kept steady and rose higher. Again I asked the African guide, "*Achi chika*?"

"Why," he said, "that is the *mutumbu*, the Jumper, the star that heralds the dawn. If you watch the place where it came up, after a while you will see the sunrise." Sure enough, shortly afterwards we saw the first streaks of dawn.

When the sun came up, we were standing on a high hill overlooking a long valley. Miles away, among the trees, I saw a curl of smoke from a place which, in Chokwe, we call *mahietu* — our home. Around noon, footsore and weary, we staggered in.

Someone has said that the morning star always comes up at the coldest, weakest, darkest, and sleepiest hour of the night, when most people are asleep, but it is always the harbinger of the dawn. I shall never forget the first time I saw it in dark Africa. Many times I have seen it since, and always it has reminded me of the Lord's promise, "Behold, I come quickly."

Organizing a School

Every mission station in Angola is required by law to do educational work. All teaching in school must be done in the Portuguese language. In elementary grades, the African vernacular may be used in oral explanation, but this must be gradually eliminated until all instruction is given in Portuguese. The object, of course, is to make the government language universal in the country. The official attitude is that the African languages are not worth preserving.

From time to time efforts were made to prohibit the printing of any literature in a Bantu language. Up until the present (1966) it is permitted to print the vernacular, if it has a Portuguese translation on the opposite page. But even this is regarded as a temporary concession. We as foreigners feel very strongly that it is a profound mistake to attempt to kill another people's language, especially when it is so beautifully constructed and so full of valuable idiom. But, being law-abiding residents and guests in a foreign land, we endeavored loyally to abide by government regulations.

As well as the three R's, emphasis is placed on practical training in school. Trades, such as carpentry, brickmaking, bricklaying, tailoring, shoemaking and repairing, and agriculture, must be taught to the African pupils. All the items in the curriculum must conform to Portuguese practice and standards of teaching. Every year each pupil must be presented for examination to a Portuguese national jury.

In 1921 these regulations regarding school work in Protestant mission schools were incorporated in Decree 77, issued by the Portuguese government. They have been strictly enforced. As a matter of fact, for many years the only educational work done specifically for Africans was done by Protestant missions, a fact almost completely ignored by official published statistics. In recent years the government has encouraged and subsidized Roman Catholic school work and corrected this anomaly. On the face of it, this decree seems moderate and wise, but the serious restriction on the use of the native languages, and the order, which forces a missionary to devote a good deal of his time to secular school work and the detailed furnishing of statistics, was a heavy blow. It also puts power into the hands of minor officials, who are often prejudiced and narrow-minded, to allow or prohibit Africans to preach the gospel in their own language.

When the decree became law, a number of missionaries left the country and crossed the border into Rhodesia or into the Congo, where there was more freedom. In some cases the native population followed them. Those who were left had to adjust their work to the new regulations.

All of the new mission workers from that time have gone to Portugal for an extended period to study the Portuguese language and Portuguese methods of education. This was necessary in order to follow the Portuguese curriculum in the schools. All the old school books were scrapped, even the Scriptures, and all literature printed in the native languages alone were prohibited. Anyone found with them in their possession was put into jail. The Bible Societies co-operated magnificently in publishing bilingual versions, although it doubled the cost of the books.

We were led to believe that if African evangelists could speak Portuguese, they would be allowed to carry on their work unhindered. Therefore every effort was made to teach them. The missionaries loyally carried out their part of the contract. But what has been the result? The general tendency has been to tighten up the screw. More and better education has been the cry. Outschool teachers were given licenses to teach, which were taken away the following year and the teachers sent home for further study.

In March 1928 another law was passed requiring all foreign missions to employ a teacher of Portuguese nationality with at least three years' training to be in charge of the school work on each station. The teacher's salary had to be paid by the missionaries. Here again the missionaries, often at great personal sacrifice, have tried to fulfill the law.

Portuguese educational methods involve a tremendous amount of paper work. Each pupil in the school has to be "matriculated." This means that a number of certificates, very difficult for an African to obtain, must be supplied. They all cost money.

Each year a jury of Portuguese officials comes round to conduct the examinations and authorize passes from one class to another. They usually stay for a week and must be entertained by the missionaries in their homes. They usually send ahead and let the senior missionary know what brand of wine they prefer with their meals. Altogether, examination week is a nightmare, both to the missionaries and to the pupils. One wonders if it is all worth while! And yet it is a small part of the price that many foreign missionaries have to pay for laboring in a land that is definitely hostile to the evangelical Protestant.

On the other hand, there is the credit side of the ledger. Perhaps no single branch of the work has paid off so handsomely in spiritual results as the school. Not a day passes but the Word of God is taught systematically and consecutively. Every day starts with a Scripture lesson. Most of the pupils spend at least three years in the classrooms. Very many have been saved during this period. Most of the men who preach and teach the Word today, were led to Christ in early life while in school. As well as this, for the first time African young people are taught punctuality, discipline, respect for authority, and personal cleanliness.

The government has encouraged and the missionaries have gladly complied in teaching trades and agriculture. By far the greatest number of carpenters, masons, bricklayers, sawyers, tailors, shoemakers, and printers in Angola have been trained in mission schools. In the early days, the missionary had to make his own furniture and build his own house. But this is no longer necessary. An African carpenter, if given a rough sketch, will do a creditable job at a reasonable price. But they need supervision, even the best of them! They are poor at initiative or invention, but good at copying a pattern.

Certain missionaries specialized in horticulture and agriculture. Mr. Sanders, of Chilonda in Bié, for many years had a citrus orchard which was without a rival in Central Africa. He experimented in budding and grafting fruit trees. A lemon will bear fruit in three years from seed, but an orange will take at least ten years. He therefore planted thousands of lemon trees and when they were ready to bear, he budded in oranges, tangerines, and grapefruit. The next year the grafts bore fruit. African young men were taught to do this work. Portuguese traders and officials from all over Angola sent in orders for trees. Not only that, but the Africans themselves caught on to the idea, with the result that in many an African's backyard, particularly in Bié, will be found a citrus orchard which has been a great factor in combating certain deficiency diseases common among the people.

In any other country, the work done by Mr. Sanders along this line would have been recognized and encouraged by the government. Instead of this, it was ignored and frequently insulting things were said to him about his garden. But he went serenely on with the work till the end of his life.

Most mission stations, as well as the regular day schools for the local people, have boarding schools for both boys and girls who come from a distance. The pupils are given the same kind of food they would have in their home villages, mostly mush and beans, with dried fish and vegetables for relish. They are given a weekly ration of salt and palm oil. Some of the oil is used in their food and some of it they rub on their skin to make it bright and shiny, a primitive form of cosmetics. Each pupil in the boarding school must pay a certain amount of money to help with his food and the expenses of the school.

In addition, several hours each day must be spent working in the fields, helping to raise food. This serves the double purpose of helping to make the school as self-supporting as pos-sible and at the same time gives opportunity to teach the pupils better methods of agriculture than they practice at home. They learn to plow with oxen broken to the yoke, to fertilize the soil, and to rotate crops.

Then there is the domestic school. In primitive Africa wom-en are married early, bear children, work in the fields, draw water, gather firewood, make clay pots, and are not sup-posed to be capable of book learning. But times are changing. Young men no longer want to marry an illiterate girl. Missionaries have encouraged the girls to come to school. For some years Naomi Cole, wife of our good friend and fellow worker, Don Cole of Detroit, had a domestic school at Chilonda. This is in addition to the regular school work. Young married women, or those en-gaged to be married, are invited to come for courses in how to run a home and take care of their children. Those unable to read are taught to read and, in addition, the gospel is preached and the Scriptures systematically expounded. This work too has re-sulted in considerable blessing.

Let it be clearly understood that the missionary in Angola, in his educational work, has a twofold obligation. First, he must fulfill government regulations in order to be allowed to stay in the country; and secondly, in order to see autonomous churches established, he must enable the people to read and understand the Scriptures. Up until recent years, government schools cater-ing alone to the education of the African were nonexistent, and those that function today are under the domination of the Ro-man Catholic church.

From the commencement of the work at Chitutu we had a school. At first the pupils had to be rounded up from the vil-lages every day. Those who came considered they were doing us a favor and wanted to be paid for coming. We had brought a supply of slates, slate pencils, blackboards, chalk, and some elementary Portuguese textbooks from Chokwe-land. Our first school was in the open air under the trees. Then the shed where we held our gospel meetings was used as a schoolroom. As time went on we got better organized, but it was some years before we achieved anything like punctuality and regular attendance.

The daily sessions always commenced with a Scripture lesson in Chokwe, usually taken from the Gospels. We went through a book like Mark or John verse by verse, explaining and applying the message to the minds of the children. The fact that we had both Chokwes and Songos in school, with two different languages and intertribal rivalry, created all kinds of problems, but at least day by day the young people were being indoctrinated with the Word of God, and at the same time being taught to read it.

Every day after roll call we had chigger drill. Chiggers are small insects, like miniature fleas, which burrow underneath the skin, usually around the toenails, and lay their eggs. They have to be dug out with a needle and the place disinfected with iodine. If allowed to stay, they form a sack, about the size of a pea, full of eggs. When this matures, the sack bursts, shedding eggs all over the ground. Each egg hatches into a chigger. We have seen African children with several toes eaten away by chiggers. When our own children were small, it was a routine chore every night to examine their toes and extract the chiggers, accompanied by many a howl and tear. It was a painful business but had to be done. Chiggers get into the feet of dogs and pigs and other animals, as well as human beings. Dogs bite them out when they can get at them, but chiggers have a habit of finding the most inaccessible places to do their irritating work, and even a domestic animal often has to have human help to get them out. So every morning in school we had chigger drill.

As the work developed we had to employ African teachers. These had to be properly qualified with a diploma for teaching Portuguese. They were usually trained in a mission school in Bié.

One of our problems among the children was pilfering and lying. But these African teachers could handle the situation much better than we could. One day a pupil reported that his money had been stolen while he was in class. The teacher gave each pupil a short piece of stick, each one the same size, and solemnly told them to take them home and bring them back the next day. Whoever stole the money, his stick would grow longer during the night. Next day one of the boys came with a piece broken off his stick. The teacher announced that he was the culprit—and sure enough he was!

School in the bush also had its diversions. One afternoon we were getting ready to dismiss, when a herdsman, who was taking care of cattle in the valley a short distance away, came rushing in to say that a lion was killing the cattle, and to come quickly. I had a rifle and a shotgun at the time. Giving the shotgun to a Songo man named Muzumbu, and taking the rifle myself, I ran with him down to the spot. We found the bull of the herd lying beside the stream with his neck broken. The claw marks were on his back and flanks where the lion had jumped on his back, and also on the side of his face where he had hit him with his mighty paw and broken his neck. The lion had then killed three good-sized calves. Two of them he had dragged into the long grass at the edge of the forest about 50 yards away. We heard his low growl as he ate one of them. I cocked the gun and went after him. He heard me coming and dropped the calf he was eating; he picked up the other one in his mouth and went off into the long grass. The sun was going in and the light was poor, so it was impossible to see him properly and get a clean shot at him. I finally had to let him go.

The Africans suggested setting a trap with the guns. They cut four forked sticks and stuck them in the ground on either side of the carcass of the calf, where he had been eating. Then they tied the guns in the forks of the sticks so that the muzzles were pointing at the carcass. Strings were attached to the triggers, passed round the forked sticks and tied to the carcass in such a way that if it was moved, the strings would discharge the guns. The boys assured me that the lion would come back.

I went back to the house and lay in bed listening for the guns to go off. I waited also all the next day, but nothing happened. On the morning of the third day we went down to the carcass. Sure enough he had come back and eaten his fill. The stomach, intestines, liver, heart, and lungs had been licked out clean. He had held the calf down while he did it and the guns were still there undischarged! He must have suspected a trap and had outwitted us.

That night, along with Muzumbu, we took a goat and tied it to a tree near the spot where the lion had eaten the calf. When the sun went down we shinnied up the tree, Muzumbu with the shotgun and I with the rifle. After a while the goat started to cry and we heard the lion roar in the distance. As he came nearer Muzumbu got the shakes and dropped his gun on the head of the goat. The frightened animal bawled piteously but the lion would not come any closer. We sat up the tree all night while at intervals the lion made the forest ring with his roars. Each time, as he stopped, we could almost hear our hearts beat as the forest was so strangely silent. Finally just before dawn, he gave us one more serenade and was gone. He played tag with us for some time and altogether, before he was shot by our missionary colleague, David Long, he had killed fourteen head of cattle.

One bright moonlight night he came again with his mate. David Long and a Songo man called Kwangu had climbed a tree beside the cattle pen and were waiting for him. As he came into the clearing and stopped, David drew a bead on him and fired. The bullet went clean through his heart and laid it in two halves. But he kept on going for some distance before he dropped. The female came back after the shot and ate a part of the hindquarters of her dead mate before dawn. It was the first time we had heard of such a thing happening.

The words "boarding school" usually give the impression of an elaborate institution with traditions of the old school tie, accessible only to the children of people in the upper income brackets. In the African bush, they simply mean a place where young people can live under African conditions, eat African food, and at the same time be free to come to school. We had boarding schools for both boys and girls. Here again there were problems. First there was the morals problem. Teenage boys and girls had to be strictly segregated and supervised outside school hours. The missionaries were responsible for behavior and discipline. This was often a 24-hours-a-day job.

Then there was the racial problem. Very often in the middle of the night there would be a tremendous rumpus with 20 or 30 girls screaming at the top of their voices. I would wearily pull out of bed and plod over to see what was going on. The dormitory had a door in the center and two shuttered windows on either side. As I knocked on the door there would be sudden silence.

Then, realizing who the intruder was, one after the other, they would nose-dive out through the open window and head for the bush. Next day there would be an inquiry. Usually it was two tribal groups fighting over some old-time feud, or over insulting remarks that had been made about one another's customs or language. We had more trouble with the girls than the boys.

Then there was the constant battle against insects. I don't think anyone can tell us anything new about ticks, bedbugs, lice, or cockroaches. We were always glad to see the army ants come. They are the scavengers and sanitary department of Central Africa. They are carnivorous. They are sometimes called soldier ants because they march in a long column often 50 feet long and six or eight abreast. The ordinary ant is 3/8ths of an inch long and deep red in color, but the scouts, that go ahead and guard the sides of the column, can be up to 3/4ths of an inch long. They have pinchers like a crab and can literally eat a person or an animal alive. It is a tragedy if they get into a pigpen or a goatpen or a chicken coop where the animals cannot get away. We have known cases where an African woman has laid her child under a tree while she worked in her field, and came back to find it covered with army ants and dead. If they come into a house, the best thing to do is get out, removing every scrap of meat or fat in the house. When they are finished, there will not be a termite, cockroach, or mouse in the place. The Umbundu name for army ants is *ovisonde* ("the bloody ones"). We were always glad to see them come into the school dormitories. They could do what any amount of insecticides could not do!

We always had a dread of epidemics among the children under our care. Africans have a natural fear of death. If two or three were to die about the same time, the people immediately think of witchcraft. In a country where smallpox, leprosy, infectious hepatitis, as well as many other fatal diseases are common, we had to be continually on the alert, and isolate the child as soon as the first symptoms appeared. On one occasion we had about a dozen boys ill at the same time with kaffir pox, which is a milder form of smallpox. My wife isolated them and herself to take care of them. One boy died. Fortunately his parents were understanding and there were no serious repercussions.

Over the years it has been a great satisfaction to see many of the young people, who went through our school, develop into leaders in the missionary work among their own people.

One of our major problems was the education of our own three children. In a pioneer field like Angola, there are no local facilities for education in the English language. This meant that when our children came to seven years of age, we were faced with the problem of their education.

We first of all tried the correspondence course sent out by the Calvert School in Baltimore, in the United States, for our oldest boy. Canada also provides correspondence courses for the children of Canadian citizens who reside overseas. These courses are excellent, and the great advantage is that the child is able to stay with his parents at an important and impressionable period of his life. Many children are constitutionally unfitted for living away from their parents for long periods in their early years. If they are forced to do this against their will, there is often an emotional upset which will leave a lasting mark on the child, which may remain through life. To carry on with a correspondence course successfully, one of the parents, at least, must give a good deal of time to it. But in our case, there were so many calls on our time that it was practically impossible to do this. Then, too, we found that a child needs the competition of other children in order to make progress. Very few missionary families have found in practical experience that the correspondence course works out.

On account of this most important problem, some missionary families have left the field permanently. After one or two terms in Africa, which are mostly spent in language study and getting to know the people, the young couple, realizing their responsibility to their growing family, give up and go home and are lost to the work. No one can judge or blame; it is a heart-breaking decision which often must be made.

We were fortunate in the fact that there was a school for missionaries' children in Northern Rhodesia (now Zambia), to which we could send our children. It was nearly a thousand miles away by road, and, in our early days, we could have them with us only for a short time in the dry season each year. But at least it was in the same country and not separated by two continents and 6,000 miles, as it would have been if we had sent them to America.

The school was started by Dr. Walter Fisher in 1926 and is located at Sakeji, in northwest Zambia, near the Congo border. The site was chosen as a central place where children from Zambia, the Congo, and Angola could come. In 1932 Mr. and Mrs. Lyndon Hess came from America and have been in charge of the school for over thirty years. They have seen it grow from very modest beginnings to a fine modern school with high standards. The first buildings were built of mud bricks with dirt floors and grass roofs. Mr. Hess is not only a qualified school principal, but a highly skilled practical man as well. All of the buildings today are of burnt brick made at the school, with cement floors, permanent roofs, and attractive furniture. At first the only illumination was oil lamps. Then came electricity, generated by a windmill. The nearby Sakeji River was dammed, and a waterwheel and a turbine installed, giving enough power for the present-day needs of the school.

There are now over 100 pupils in residence. The school takes care of the primary grammar school education, but the pupils have to go further afield for high school. Some go to Chingola on the Copper Belt or to Bulawayo or Salisbury in Rhodesia for this.

We personally, like many other missionaries, are very grateful for the devoted and faithful service of Mr. and Mrs. Hess and their capable band of teachers at Sakeji, who carry on this difficult task of the education of our children, and in this way free many parents for their missionary activities.

Medical Work

In addition to educational work, Decree 77, issued by the Portuguese government, also insisted that every mission station must offer medical assistance to the Africans, either in a dispensary or hospital with qualified personnel. Detailed statistics of this work must be furnished to the government in an annual report.

A clause in the law promised subsidies for school and medical work, if these were carried out according to government standards. As a matter of fact this was never honored. No government help of any kind was ever offered or received. Heavy duties were often levied on drugs brought in from abroad to be used in treating sick Africans.

From the beginning of our pioneer efforts among the Songo people at Chitutu we tried to help the people when they were sick or injured. In those days our nearest doctor or hospital was more than 200 miles away and the only way to get there was on foot. The government had no organized medical service in these isolated regions. As a matter of fact, we often took care of lonely government officials when they had malaria or blackwater fever.

At first the people were afraid to accept our medicine and were threatened by the witch doctors of the dire consequences of coming near us. Infant mortality was terribly high. The people had no idea that malaria was carried by mosquitoes or that bilharzia was contracted by contaminated water. Their huts were breeding places of ticks, lice, bedbugs, and other forms of filthy insect life. Leprosy was very common and the person who contracted the disease was not segregated but ate and slept with the other members of the family. Smallpox and a milder form called kaffir pox frequently decimated whole villages. A very high percentage of the population was infected with some form of intestinal worms. This, of course, was the result of their unclean habits in preparing and handling food. Conjunctivitis, a highly contagious eye disease, swept the country every dry season. Children especially suffered from it. It was carried from one to the other by flies. Another common ailment was large tropical ulcers, usually on the front of the leg, which were particularly difficult to heal.

We had no pretentions to being experts, but at least we knew more than the ignorant witch doctors or their gullible patients. The drugs and remedies that helped ourselves and kept us in health, we knew would help them. As time went on we built a dispensary and equipped it with the common remedies and with the new wonder antibiotic drugs as they came along. As the people got to know us, and that we had no ulterior motive but a genuine desire to help, prejudice and fear were gradually broken down and the people came to the dispensary in increasing numbers. Over the years we accumulated a fairly extensive medical library, so that by reading and experience knowledge increased. My wife did the medical work, while I did the teeth extractions.

On our first and subsequent furloughs, a dentist friend gave me the opportunity of getting some training and on our return to Africa provided me with the necessary instruments. Hardly a day passed that there weren't four or five people there to have teeth extracted. No anaesthesia was used, but if anyone was anxious to have an injection of cocaine, he paid for it. Otherwise the extraction was free. On trips around the villages, I always took dental forceps along and was often stopped at the roadside by people with a tooth-ache. One day an African elder wanted all his teeth extracted as he was anxious to have artificial dentures. He really needed to have them all out as they were hopelessly decayed. He sat on the ground while I extracted nine teeth without any anaesthetic.

"Well, maybe you have had enough," I suggested.

"No, *Nala*," he said, "I want them all out." I pulled four-teen teeth altogether, some of them difficult stumps, and he never made a sound or groan.

Epilepsy was very common. Many times people were brought to us who had been terribly burned by rolling over on top of the fire in their hut while in an epileptic fit. These cases took months of daily care and after they were healed it often would reoccur as they went back again to sleep in their huts under the same conditions.

Leprosy is very widespread in practically every part of Angola. Most of the mission stations have a camp where lepers live for a period of two years while they are under treatment. In the olden days they were given injections of chalmarooga oil, but in more recent years, one of the new wonder drugs, diazone, was used with spectacular results. Owing to the fact that lepers had to stay for a two-year course of treatment and constantly heard the gospel during that time, very many of these afflicted people became real Christians and in turn ministered to their own people. After we left Chitutu in the Songo country for Capango in Bié, our fellow workers and successors at Chitutu, Mr. and Mrs. Jack King, continued to work among lepers and saw considerable results, not only in restored bodies but in spiritually transformed lives. The ravages and deformities caused by leprosy can never be repaired, but at least the disease can be arrested by this marvelous drug and become inactive.

As well as the dispensaries on each mission station in Angola, later came two fine hospitals, one at Boma in Chokwe-land, which was built and developed by Dr. Leslie Bier from Brantford, Ontario; and another at Monte Esperança, near to Coemba, about 50 miles east of the Quanza River on the Benguela railway, built by Dr. Ross Woodward of Toronto, Canada. Dr. Bier is a very fine surgeon and over a period of thirty-five years has saved countless thousands of lives. He also trained a large number of African orderlies and nurses, some of whom became valuable helpers in the medical work in various mission stations. Hazel Kennan from Dublin, Ireland, and Vivian Grant from London, Ontario, both registered nurses, rendered invaluable service for many years in the hospital at Boma. Miss Kennan died in 1967. Dr. Woodward and Charles Shorten of London, Ontario, built up a fine hospital work at Monte Esperança. In both these hospitals an extensive leper work was carried on.

Owing to the fighting in Eastern Angola in 1967 the hospitals have had to be closed down and the personnel evacuated. The future of this most valuable work, which has been so greatly blessed in the past, is uncertain.

The hospitals at Boma and at Monte Esperança were too far away from where we lived to be of any service in an emergency. When we lived at Capango in Bié, our nearest hospital was at Chissamba about 40 miles away. This was in charge of Dr. Walter Strangway, a Canadian missionary from Simcoe, Ontario. Dr. Strangway had a marvelous reputation both among the Portuguese and the Africans as a surgeon and a friend. Very many times, at all hours of the day and night, we had to call on him for help in an emergency. Not only was his skill and help freely bestowed upon Africans, but many of our missionaries owe their lives to this most devoted and gracious man. His wife, Alice, is a qualified pathologist and is a capable and dedicated collaborator with her husband in his service to the Africans and to the whole country. Their home was always open to those who were ill and needing care. The hospital at Chissamba is a tribute to the lifetime work of this distinguished couple.

In all our years of giving medical assistance to Africans, we never attempted major surgery. We were cautious and knew our limitations, but many times by force of circumstances were obliged to do things which would be considered presumptuous in a civilized community. It was either do something or let the person die.

Sometimes we had the help of African nurses who had been trained in a hospital. One of these was Feliciano. He was full of self-confidence but, unlike the missionary, did not know where to stop.

On one occasion, while sleeping in a native hut, my wife was bitten by a tick. Her arm swelled up and she needed an intravenous injection of a remedy without delay. I had made several attempts to insert the needle into a deeply buried vein, without success. But Feliciano, who happened to be in the village at the time, was successful at the first try.

On another occasion, a woman wrapped in a blanket, was brought in a truck by a Portuguese trader and laid on the ground on our front porch.

"Please take care of her," said the trader, and drove off. The African woman had been in childbirth for several days. The unborn child had been dead for some time. There was no doctor available and our hearts sank. But then Feliciano turned up.

"Don't worry, *Ndona*," he said, "I will take care of this." We carried the woman over to the dispensary. Feliciano produced a towel and a cake of carbolic soap and scrubbed up like a professional surgeon. Then he prayed as he had seen the missionary doctor do, and started. He delivered the child in about half an hour. We kept out of his way while he worked.

Another day a man turned up at the local government post with a healed scar across his abdomen. The official asked him where he got it. The man replied, "Feliciano." Apparently he had opened the man's abdomen.

As we see it, this is the danger in turning African nurses loose in native villages to do medical work without proper supervision. While the missionary knows his limitations and does not charge for his services, sooner or later the natives yield to the temptation to overcharge their fellow Africans just as the witch doctor did in the olden days. It was not long before Feliciano had a motorcycle and many other of the ex-pensive gadgets of the white man.

In recent years the question has sometimes been asked, in view of the changing conditions in many countries and the takeover by communistic regimes: is it wise for evangelical missions to sink large sums of money in hospitals and other humanitarian work? This of course is a legitimate question, but as far as Angola is concerned, the law required the missionary to do this type of work, and, like school work, it has been very greatly blessed in winning the confidence of the people and in opening doors and hearts to the gospel. The money spent in this way has been a good investment which has paid rich dividends in spiritual results. But some of the new regimes in Africa today are willing and anxious to receive the benefits of medical and educational work, but frown upon and in some cases even prohibit its use in the propagation of the gospel. We personally feel that the spiritual side is of paramount importance. Social work is important but every time should be associated with and subjugated to the spiritual.

Witch Doctor

 My first contact with witchcraft and ritual murder was in Bié, three months after arriving in Angola. A man had been killed and his body strung up by the head and feet in the branches of a tree. The raw white man, just out from home, is apt to laugh at the superstition and fears of the African, who wears a small antelope horn tied to a string round his neck, and who offers sacrifice to an image stuck in the ground outside his house. But he has every right to be afraid; mysterious things happen which cannot be accounted for on any rational basis.

Over the years the white man learns to reserve his judgment and usually comes to the conclusion that sinister forces are at work, which the Christian recognizes as the powers of darkness. When I asked an African for an explanation of some weird happening, he would usually shrug his shoulders and reply, "*Ngana*, you don't understand." And truly I didn't. It was only after many years of intimate contact with the people, in every phase of their lives, that I began to understand a little of the kingdom of darkness. First of all, there is the infiltration of communistic propaganda with its insinuation that the white missionary is the agent of western imperialism and that he has opened the door to all the abuses that have plagued the African continent for one hundred years. This of course is completely untrue. The record shows that the missionary has always been in the vanguard of true progress and enlightenment. Then there has been in many places a return to witchcraft and pagan custom. Even some African leaders with a university education are openly advocating this.

In African life religion and medicine are inseparably associated. When an African dies his spirit becomes an *ochilulu*. It stays around the village and has the power to enter into people and objects, and if angry or peeved can cause all kinds of sickness and trouble. For this reason the spirits must be pacified.

The often repeated statement that Africans are animists, worshippers of inanimate objects, is not strictly accurate. The African makes an idol, it is true, to which he bows down and prays. He also builds an altar, on which he sprinkles the blood of animals and fowls, and on which he places small offerings of meal and meat. But it is not to the piece of stick or stone or clay that he prays. The spirits of his ancestors are believed to come and inhabit these things, and it is to them that he prays. He does not worship, in our sense of the term, but simply brings an offering or sprinkles the blood in an effort to keep an angry spirit quiet, so that it will do him no harm. Prayers are usually said at night when the spirits are supposed to gather. This is done about every two weeks. A plate of meal is placed beside the image when the prayer is offered. When a spirit has become friendly, instead of malignant, it is called a *hamba*.

The spirit most greatly to be feared is that of a newly-born child which died at birth. It has been deprived of the realization of a full life and is therefore angry. The same can be said of the spirits of the insane. The spirits are believed to have their abode beneath the ground and are called by the Chokwe *akwamwishi*, meaning "those from below." Horns, images, and hollow seeds, which are hung around the neck or tied to the wrist, are not idols, but charms or amulets, made and blessed by the witch doctor, and are supposed to keep away danger or bring children to barren women. They correspond to the rabbit's feet or lucky charms worn by some so-called civilized people.

Next to the chief, the most influential man in African life is the witch doctor. Dugald Campbell in his book on Africa, *In the*

Heart of Bantuland, describes twelve kinds of witch doctors. He is priest, spirit medium, doctor, rain maker, herbalist, and interpreter of dreams—all in one. As a diviner he is called a *chimbanda*, and as a healer a *mbuki*, from *ku-wuka* ("to heal"). Both men and women may become witch doctors. Through the aid of the familiar spirit he utters oracles, officiates as priest in the worship of demons, "smells out" criminals with the aid of the divining basket, and prescribes herbal medicines for the sick. At his initiation he agrees to become the slave of the demon for life. He literally sells his soul in return for his power.

One of the witch doctor's main functions is the detection of people who are practicing sorcery, but in addition he is consulted about a thousand other things. There is no stigma attached to his profession; on the contrary, the people regard him as the protector of society. Usually he is a neurotic character with a predisposition to see visions and vivid dreams. To do his work, he almost invariably falls into a trance and is extraordinarily susceptible to psychic influences. There does not seem to be any doubt that he often has genuine contact with supernatural satanic forces. I have seen and heard witch doctors, when in a trance, speak in languages which they ordinarily do not know. When asked about it afterwards, they say it is their familiar spirit which speaks through them. At the same time the witch doctor is unusually clever, with keen powers of observation and mother wit. He has a wide repertoire of sleight-of-hand tricks which are often used to hoodwink the gullible people.

A witch doctor usually has a training period lasting about two years. Before that, he has had a "call." This generally is the result of a series of mysterious illnesses. When the sick one consults a witch doctor, he is told that the spirit of one of his ancestors wants to take possession of him, so that he might become a diviner. The first step is to organize a hunt for the spirit. If the initiate kills an antelope, that is a good omen. But he literally has to give himself body and soul to the spirit seeking possession.

Materially it is a costly business. The witch doctor initiating the neophyte has to be paid at every step. First an advance fee of ten fowls; then four yards of cloth for leaving his village. To make him hurry, he receives the gift of a roasting pig. The diving basket costs an ox; the articles in it cost a goat; the price for mixing the medicines which give power to them is eight yards of cloth. And this is only the beginning. At every stage of the ceremony fees have to be paid.

During the two years' apprenticeship the neophyte learns about herbal medicines and poisons. Therein lies the danger: he can both kill and cure. In order to provide the female complement to the spirit of the divining basket, he invites a girl to spend the night with him; in the morning he gives her a poisoned cloth, which causes her illness and death. Her spirit will assist the one he already has in interpreting the omens of the divining basket. In order to attract influential people, the diviner may kill a child with poison. The body is buried, but later he digs it up secretly, takes off the scalp and wraps it in a little cloth. This is laid in the bottom of the divining basket.

In the African's mind, sickness is the result of one of four causes: evil spirits; witchcraft; a bad condition of the blood; parasites in the abdomen, generally called the animal or the worm. When a person is taken ill with a sickness which re-fuses to respond to ordinary treatment, or some mysterious calamity overtakes an individual or a village, a witch doctor is consulted. He, first of all, divines to find out the nature of the trouble, and then prescribes the remedy. He has a little rattle, made of a hollow gourd about the size of an apple, with a short stick thrust through it and a few small pebbles inside to make it rattle. With this he rings up the spirit world.

His divining basket is a flat tray woven out of reeds, and on this he has an odd collection of chicken bones, a coin, an image carved out of wood, some part of a human body, generally a bone, an antelope horn, a chief's inheritance ring, a miniature pounding stick and mortar. Practically everything connected with native life is symbolically represented. Each article has a specific meaning which all the people understand. The antelope horn means a man's voice, the image represents the spirits, the coin means wealth, the pounding stick and mortar stand for food or its preparation, the chief's ring signifies something connected with authority, the human bone, witchcraft. With a deft twist of the basket, the diviner throws its contents up, like a boy tossing pennies, and their position, as they fall into the basket, tells him the mind of the spirits. Whichever object comes up prominently, each time the basket is shaken, gives him a clue to the cause of the trouble. If it is the spirits, he proceeds to diagnose which kind of a spirit it is that is causing the trouble.

As well as the basket, some diviners consult the spirits by means of a mirror or in the reflections in water. They work by a process of suggestion and elimination. The people sit around in a circle, keeping up a singsong chant in a monotonous tone, while the drums beat in rhythm. A series of questions are asked, either by the diviner himself or by one of his assistants. When he hits on the right clue, the song suddenly rises up to a crescendo; if he gets off on a wrong tack, it dies down again. He follows this up until he arrives at the correct answer.

The witch doctors are guilty of much deception and trickery, and line their pockets at the expense of the credulous people. But at the same time, as in modern spiritism, there is no doubt that at times they have genuine contact with the underworld of demons. When divining they often go into a hypnotic trance and speak in a deep unnatural voice, the air around them seems charged with satanic power. This is evident to anyone who has lived with it for many years. Demon possession is very common in a pagan society. Women seem to be more susceptible to this than men. Many times we have seen both men and women under the power of evil spirits, which has left no doubt in our mind that demon possession is a reality and is not merely hysteria or epilepsy or insanity, but rather is a genuine contact with the powers of darkness.

The diviners differentiate many kinds of spirits, corresponding to the various types of disease, each one with a different kind of treatment. Here are the names in Chokwe of half a dozen, and the witch doctor's procedure to effect a cure:

Musangi. This is the spirit of a slave whose body, when he died, was thrown out into the bush without burial and with-out any ceremony to appease the spirit. It is therefore angry and has caused the sickness. The sick man makes a heap of earth beside the altar, puts a mush paddle stick standing on one end in the center, and ties a green leaf on top. Manioc meal is sprinkled on the altar.

Pupa. This spirit causes fever pains in arms, legs, and head. An altar is built and an axhead suspended from it. A stick with three forks at the top is stuck in the ground, and a gourd placed in the forks. The face of the sick person is smeared with red and white clay, as is also the axshaft.

Mufti. This is literally "the dead man." If after a person dies, a number of others in the village die or are very ill, a witch doctor is called in. After divining, he announces that the first person to die went to the grave with anger in his heart. They all then go to the cemetery, the grave is opened, and the corpse exposed. A fowl is strangled and thrown to the body. Some mush is made out of the outside parings of the manioc root, and this, along with some beer, is put in his mouth. A piece of mud is slapped on the crown of his head. The grave is then filled in and all go back to the village and drum all night. As soon as the day dawns, all go to the crossroads leading to the graveyard, carrying a few clay pots and some ashes. A shallow hole is dug in a sweet potato patch and the ashes placed in the bottom. The pots are placed on top of the ashes and earth heaped around, almost to the lips of the pots. This prevents the spirit coming again to the village to do any more damage. The witch doctor is paid a heavy fee for his work.

Ngombo. If a person dies and the relatives fail to appease the spirit, it is angry and someone is taken seriously ill. The men go hunting and if possible kill an antelope. An altar is built beside the door of the hut of the sick person and the blood of the antelope is sprinkled on it. The raw liver is put on a plate, offered on the altar, and then is eaten by the diviner. The skull of the antelope is impaled on a stick beside the altar.

Chisola. The spirit of a child. If a woman's children die, one after another in infancy, she ties a number of little sticks together, with a small mop of cotton attached to one end. The mop is plastered with red clay and tied round her neck. This is a charm to bring other children. The most vindictive spirits are those of children. Young children are buried in a graveyard by themselves. No one goes there, because if the spirit of a child takes possession of a person, the possessed one never recovers. The child has been deprived of going through life and leaving posterity and is therefore angry. To keep the spirit away, a live fowl is taken to the altar and prayers said, but the fowl is not killed.

Makongo. If an African has a jerky leg or arm, the witch doctor brews some medicine and mixes it with castor oil. With this he anoints the body of the sick person. He brings a cord and crosses it on the back or chest of the patient, from the shoulder to the opposite armpit. This cord is never thrown away. In an effort to exorcise the spirit, the villagers sing and drum all night. When the spirit comes out, the sick man's body jerks violently. If, after trying the remedy prescribed, there is no improvement, then they resort to the *hamba liakwanda.* This corresponds to the "unknown god" of the Athenians. It is the unknown spirit and all kinds of efforts and sacrifices are made to appease it.

Another outstanding cause of sickness is witchcraft. A person can be bewitched in various ways. Certain evil-disposed individuals are said to cut out a section of the large bone of the lower leg of a dead man, and push out the marrow so that it forms a tube. The person who wishes to bewitch his neighbor then buys some gunpowder and goes off to a remote place in the bush. He catches a number of reptiles and insects, that have a poisonous sting or bite, such as a snake, scorpion, hornet, bee, wasp, and various kinds of ants. These are all roasted together and reduced to a powder. He then goes to the village and prepares his "gun." The mixture is put inside the bone and a little gunpowder placed at one end. He strikes a match and, as he lights the gunpowder, he points the gun at the house of the person he wishes to kill, at the same time mentioning his name. When the gun goes off with a pop, the doomed man is believed to feel a stab in his side. Unless a powerful witch doctor is consulted, and the poison extracted by cutting and cupping, the person is supposed to die.

Sometimes a person is killed by poison and the heart extracted, in order to make another type of gun. This is set by the side of a path and is supposed to go off as the doomed person passes by. We know personally of two cases where a man was killed to get his heart to make this magic gun. One of these was a white man. He was enticed out of his house at night, by a party of Africans, and waylaid and killed. The other was a chief who lived near us, who killed his own brother for the same purpose.

There is another fraternity of wizards who use the human eye, which they extract from the body of a person they have killed, and which is used for witchcraft. In 1926 a young man, who was one of the carriers of my wife's hammock on the journey from Bié to Chokweland, was suddenly taken ill and died. Some of the missionaries went to the village to attend the burial. They found the body completely wrapped in bark cloth. Suspecting foul play, they asked that the wrappings be removed. At first they were refused but, on demanding that it be done, they found that one eye had been gouged out and a finger cut off the body. A human eye is supposed to be a very powerful fetish. Members of the fraternity are said to meet each other and carry on their deliberations in the depths of the forest at the dead of night.

Another popular method of killing an enemy is to drop poison or a poisoned thorn on or near his doorstep. In some cases the poison is said to work through the skin and kill the person without any actual wound. At other times poison is dropped in the food or in the water gourd. If anyone is accused of killing or injuring another by witchcraft, he must take the poison test.

These ideas may sound queer and even ridiculous to civilized people, but we have seen some very weird things happen. Some of them could be explained by autosuggestion or fright on the part of the people who thought themselves be-witched, but others we confess baffle explanation.

The third cause of illness, in an African's mind, is a wrong condition of the blood. When a black man turns a pale color, it is suspected that his blood is out of order. Someone touches the palm of the sick man's hand with his tongue, and it is said that he can tell if the blood is poor by the taste! A person trained for the job then comes and makes a quick cut in the artery at the side of his head. As the blood spurts, the per-son often faints. When the witch doctor decides that enough blood has been let, he quickly binds the wound with a piece of barkrope and something hard over the actual cut. The patient is given a plentiful supply of food to build him up.

Cupping is very frequently employed for inflammation and for certain kinds of pain. The "cup" is sometimes a small antelope horn and sometimes a diminutive gourd. Small cuts are made in the skin and the cup, with a hole in the bottom, clamped over the wound. All the air is then sucked out of the cup and a piece of beeswax quickly pushed into the hole. The vacuum draws the blood out of the wound. Cupping is also resorted to for snake bite. It would be difficult to find an African, in the more primitive parts of Africa, who has no cupping marks on his body.

Nearly all stomach disorders are attributed to "the worm." An African will describe very minutely the travels of this animal all over his insides and imitate the weird noises it can make. His trouble is mostly gas pains but he would not believe you if you told him so. On the other hand, a very large percentage of the people really are infected with worms of one kind or another. In the native mind the great remedy for all these disorders is either to kill the worm with something bitter, or else get rid of the trouble by vomiting. Anyone with a plentiful supply of Epsom salts or a potent emetic can make his reputation in Africa as a doctor in a very short time.

Then there is the witch doctor's treatment in accidents. In bone fractures, a little mat is made of thin strips of bamboo woven together with bark string. The bone is carefully set and this mat is tied around the part to act as a splint. When the bone has started to knit, a goat is killed and the contents of its stomach mixed with leaves taken from a river valley. The fractured part is massaged daily with this mixture for some time. In the case of a compound fracture, where large bones protrude through the skin, we know of one case where a small hardwood dowel was whittled down and one end pushed into the marrow of the bone. The other end was then inserted into the other bone and the whole tied up as in a simple fracture. This man had a running sore for a long time but it finally healed.

A favorite salve for ulcers is the inner bark of the wild plum tree, pounded into a pulp and plastered on the sore. Sometimes a castor oil leaf is put on an open sore as a dressing.

In diseases of the eye cupping is usually resorted to, this being done on the temples. Some witch doctors get a human eye, boil it up with certain leaves, and strain the mixture. This is then dropped in people's eyes to cure inflammation, etc.

Other witch doctors employ a kind of holy water to cure the sick. To make this, a piece of human flesh or bone (called *Kau*) is dropped into a pot of water with some leaves. This is boiled and strained and used for anointing. For headache, a string is tied tightly around the head at the level of the temples.

An African once told us what, in the native mind, causes goiter. He said that white people usually boil and strain their drinking water and therefore never have goiter! The African drinks unclean water with dirt and insects in it. These all stick in their neck causing the goiter. It is just as simple as that!

We have seen native women give enemas to their children by means of a large straw. They use warm water in which leaves with a mintlike smell have been infused.

Then, primitive Africa has its chiropractors. I have seen African carriers, after a long exhausting journey, who have carried 60-pound loads on their heads all day, lie flat on their stomachs, while one of their number walks up and down their bare backs, manipulating their vertebrae with his toes. They say that this relieves the tiredness.

There is some evidence that witch doctors inoculated for smallpox before it was practiced in Europe. They simply made a cut in the wrist and rubbed some of the crust from a smallpox sore into the wound. Sometimes it resulted in a full scale case of smallpox, but usually it worked like an inoculation, a few days of fever and then immunity.

An important part of the witch doctor's work is the administration of the poison test. If a person dies suddenly under mysterious circumstances, a diviner is called in. If, after divining, he says that the person has been killed by sorcery, the relatives immediately set about finding the guilty party. Two young men are sent off, generally some distance away, to a well-known witch doctor, who proceeds to "smell out," by means of the divining basket, the name of the culprit. The diviner is usually a sly cunning old man, who knows most of the people in the village from which the messengers have come. By carefully observing the faces of the young men, as he mentions all the names of the people he knows, he finds out whom they have in mind as the slayer of the dead man. He then triumphantly announces his name. He is then paid for his services and the messengers start back to their village.

On arrival the messengers tell the headman secretly what they have learned. Everyone is then assembled in the center of the village. The headman carries red and white chalk and goes around marking everyone not implicated in the crime with white chalk. When the accused man is reached, he is marked with the red chalk. He is immediately placed by himself and must not return to his house. He sleeps in the open palaver shed and can eat raw manioc and peanuts, but not the usual mush.

Two other messengers are set off to obtain the bark of a certain tree, from which the poison for the ordeal is prepared. Certain villages own one of these trees and a goat is paid for some of the bark. The bark is cut up into small pieces, pounded in a mortar, and soaked in cold water. The mixture has both emetic and purgative properties and causes death if enough is taken. The accused person is kept fasting the night previous to the ordeal.

In the early morning everyone goes to a rendezvous in the bush. A long-shaped mound is prepared, about the size and shape of a newly filled-in grave. Alongside, a booth of tree branches and leaves has been built, in which squats the man who will administer the poison. He hides his head as the accused passes, and growls, "Who am I?" The accused must answer immediately and tell his name; if not, the other curses him and says he will die.

The accused person now sits on the prepared mound and the people arrange themselves in two groups, one on either side of the mound, the friends of the accused on the one side and his foes on the other. The people all firmly believe that if the man is guilty of the crime he will die, but if innocent, the poison is powerless to injure him. If he refuses to take the poison, he is immediately killed with an ax. When he has drunk the poison, his enemies start to shout, "Die, die," and curse him. His friends shout, "Don't die, don't die," and encourage him. If he vomits the poison, there is much hand clapping and singing on the part of his partisans, and all return to the village. If his eyes start to roll and he falls over, his enemies rush in to finish him off with the pounding stick and mortar in which the poison was mixed.

Those who are afraid run away; the others cut off his clothing, which is given to the person who administered the poison. The mortar is tied around his neck with his belt. Firewood and dead branches are gathered and heaped around the corpse, and the whole set on fire. The people sit up all night and beat the drums to drive away the spirit. The witch doctor is then paid a heavy fee for his services.

Many disappear in this way, some of whom we have known personally. We have been present and seen the bodies just after they were killed. The poison ordeal is banned by the Portuguese government, but it takes place frequently without its coming to the knowledge of the authorities. It is usually administered in an isolated place in the depths of the forest and the Africans responsible are careful to cover up all evidence of the crime. If it does come to the ears of officialdom, the case is gone into by the local Portuguese administrator and those found guilty are generally given a term of imprisonment and banished to another part of Africa. The Portuguese criminal code does not permit capital punishment!

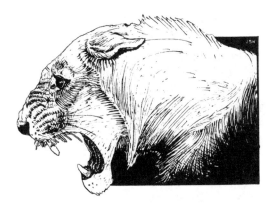

Travel de Luxe

In our early days in Angola, I never dreamed that I would ever own an automobile. That was the rich man's toy. Those were the days of footslogging; 20 miles a day was a good day's journey and one usually ended by sleeping on the ground at night, beside a fire, under the stars. There was an attraction about the life. We had time to stop at every village, dicker with the women for a chicken for our supper, and gossip the gospel with the elders in the *chota* (palaver house) at night.

Some of the Portuguese traders used a riding ox or a *tipoia*. This latter was a hammock slung on a palmpole and carried on the shoulders of two sweating Africans, stripped to the waist. Mentally I despised this form of travel. It was all right for a woman or a sick man, but not for an able-bodied man with two healthy legs.

Some missionaries tried donkeys as transport animals, but with limited success. They were constantly getting lost and attracted hungry lions to the camp at night.

In over thirty-five years in Angola I have seen only one horse. It was a weak and sickly-looking beast. The tsetse fly is found in some areas, and this may be the reason why the Portuguese have not used horse transport in the country. The tsetse fly is the carrier of sleeping sickness and attacks both man and beast. The horse seems to be especially vulnerable.

A Boer colony in the Huila district introduced the Boer wagon, which was extensively used in South Africa by the Voortrekers (Boer pioneers), but by and large, the usual method of transport, up until the late twenties, was the African porter with his 60-pound load, painfully covering 20 miles a day.

A practical invention of the missionaries in Angola was the bushcar, called by the Ovimbundu the *alikoke*. It was a contraption like a rickshaw, but with only one wheel. Over the wheel was balanced a basketwork or plywood chair on springs, and a pair of steel tubular shafts, which projected before and behind. Two Africans, one pulling in front and one pushing behind, propelled the thing along the winding tortuous 9-inch paths through the forest or across the plains. When the road was good, they could run about 8 miles an hour. The wheel was usually from a motorcycle and had a pneumatic tire. Traders would sometimes borrow the bushcar, and I have seen some who carried a *jambok* (hippohide whip) under the seat, which they didn't mind using if the Africans didn't run fast enough!

It was in the twenties that the automobile appeared. This meant the enormous task of making roads. The first roads were usually made by the military, using native labor to do the work. Those were the days when there were no bulldozers or power saws or roadmaking equipment of any kind. The work people were recruited by force by native soldiers in the villages, and made to work for many weeks and even months on end. They received no pay and had to provide their own food and tools. The men used their small native axes to cut down the trees and grub out the roots, while the women and children, who also worked, cut down the undergrowth and grass with their small hoes, about the size of a man's hand, and carried gravel and anthill dirt in their food baskets to fill up the holes and do the grading.

Africans more skilled with the ax had to cut hardwood sticks for building bridges across the rivers and streams. Each village had to provide its quota for this forced unpaid labor, and those headmen who were slow at furnishing the required number of workers were beaten with the *palmatorio* or hippohide whip or else put in prison. (A *palmatorio* is an instrument of torture shaped like a large wooden spoon. Sometimes holes are bored in the bowl of the spoon to cause suction. When a person is beaten on the palms of the hands with this wooden instrument, the hands swell up like balls. The ends of the fingers are apt to burst. For good measure, sometimes the victim is beaten on the soles of the feet as well.) Those in prison were not fed. Relatives had to bring their food to them or they would die of starvation. The building of roads in Angola cost an enormous toll in human lives.

After the roads were built, they required constant care. Every few weeks the lush undergrowth had to be scraped off and fresh gravel laid down. In the dry season bush fires burned out the stick bridges, and in the wet season floods and heavy rains washed out deep ruts and gullies in the dirt roads. Next morning the soldier with his whip would inevitably appear with the request or demand for road workers. This system has gone on for many years. Around the towns at the coast and along the railroad an effort is being made to build better roads, and we understand that these will be paid for. But up until 1961, when the trouble erupted in the northwest, the old system still carried on in most parts of the country. It was one of the factors that caused the trouble.

We bought our first car in 1931. It was a Ford Model A pick-up. We worked it hard for seven years and it gave excel-lent service. On one occasion we almost lost it in the Quanza River. We were bringing a sick African child out to Bié, to try to find medical help. The road between Capunda and the Quanza River was new and it had rained heavily. In the distance of about 50 miles we sank to the axles twenty-three times. Each time we had to cut branches of trees and lay them on the road, to give traction to the wheels, jack the car up out of the mud, fill in the holes with clods and grass, and try again.

Actually we were three days negotiating the 50 miles. We had taken only one day's food supply with us, but the morning we started before dawn I had shot a rabbit, and it, along with native mush, helped out. We slept the two nights at the roadside, in native huts infested with ticks and bedbugs. The mosquitoes, too, kept up a constant attack from sunset till dawn.

Then we came to the Quanza, a river at this point about 600

yards broad, with no bridge or pontoon and a swiftly racing current. There were three or four large dugout canoes at the crossing. These we placed side by side, put some planks transversely on top and lashed them together with barkrope to make a pontoon. A native paddler stepped into the bow and stern of each canoe. Then we ran the car on board and blocked the wheels.

About half a mile downstream was a series of rapids and, when we were about halfway across, the full force of the current caught us and sucked us inevitably towards them. The African paddlers panicked and stopped paddling. Disaster seemed certain. I jumped from one dugout to the other, thumped the terrified paddlers on their bare backs, yelling at them to get on with it, and finally they got down to work. Only just in time. We finally made it. A Portuguese trader who watched us helplessly from the bank, told us he thought we had lost the car, and of course we would have gone with it.

The nearest point where auto repairs could be done was at Malange, about 200 miles away, so I had to do most of the work myself. I learned mechanics the hard way. Nearly every trip resulted in a broken spring or a crack in the chassis or body work. Hidden stumps on the road covered with under-growth tore lumps out of the sidewalls of the tires.

But the worst experience came from the maliciousness of a Portuguese trader, who wanted to do a mean trick on a fellow trader. Our second car was a V-8 Ford pickup, which I bought secondhand from a fellow missionary. When he delivered it, I asked him to bring an eighty-gallon drum of gasoline. The place where he bought it was over 600 miles away by road.

As my missionary friend was leaving, I said, "If anything goes wrong with this bus, I don't know what I'll do, as I have never seen the inside of a V-8 motor." He smiled and replied, "You won't be long until you know all about it!" This was verily true!

On the first trip, I filled the tank with gas from the drum. About 40 miles from home the motor seized. I always carried a kit of mechanic's tools in the car. When the starter failed to turn the motor over and the starting handle also could not rotate, I decided to have a look inside the motor. On removing one of the cylinder heads, I saw that the inside looked as if someone had taken a bucket of molasses or chewed toffee and spilled it all over the works.

It was evident that nothing could be done at the roadside, so I replaced the cylinder head and recruited some Africans to push the car home. The road was full of holes and covered with deep sand, the country too was hilly, and it was back-breaking work to push it up the steep grades. After some miles we met a man with a wagon pulled by eight yoke of oxen. He very kindly agreed to unhitch his wagon. We attached the drag chain to the front bumper of the car, and had the humiliation of arriving back home pulled by sixteen long-horned oxen!

Next day I got to work and dismantled the motor. Every part was carefully laid out on the bench and a diagram made of where it came from. Each item was then cleaned and soaked in kerosene and put back in its place. When the motor was re-assembled, the tank was once again filled with gas, and off we went in the opposite direction.

But the same thing happened all over again. This time, as well as cleaning up the motor, I took out the gas tank and the fuel lines and thoroughly flushed them out. I had never heard of anyone dropping sugar in the gasoline. I had heard of sand and bullrushes and water—but sugar! I am ashamed to admit it, but before I discovered the source of the trouble, I had taken the head off the motor eight times. Then a Portuguese mechanic let me into the secret. Anyone who wants to make an enemy really uncomfortable drops sugar in his gasoline.

Two years later I met the man who sold the gasoline to my friend, who passed it on innocently to me. The trader had meant it for an entirely different party! In compensation he gave me a new drum of eighty gallons of gas. I consoled myself with the reflection that at least the experience had taught me the inner workings of a Ford V-8 motor.

Standard equipment for travel with an automobile in the wet season in Angola is a shovel for digging mud, an ax for cutting down tree branches, two good jacks, a piece of plank for putting under them, and a block and tackle for anchoring to a tree and pulling the car out of a hole. A modern low-slung sedan is practically useless on the dirt and sand roads of the interior. The ideal vehicle is a jeep or LandRover with a four-wheel drive and a power winch in front.

A modern railway now crosses Angola from Lobito to Teixeira de Sousa, on the frontier with the Congo. From there it connects with the line to Elizabethville and Capetown. In living memory the journey across Angola was a perilous adventure. Now it can be done in less than twenty-four hours in a train with beds and a restaurant car. There is also an efficient air service, linking Luanda and Lobito with Silva Porto and Luso in the interior.

The Mailman

To a missionary in an isolated place in a foreign land, the most welcome sight is the arrival of the mail-man with his most precious burden of news from the home-land. In the early days, a letter sent from one part of the country to another was taken by a messenger on foot. A piece of stick was split part way down the middle, the letter inserted, and the split end of the stick tied with a string. The messenger was called *mukwamukanda* ("he of the letter"). He was literally a walking epistle. He was! As an important individual, bearer of the white man's message, he was royally entertained and directed on his way in every village as he went along.

For many years we received mail from overseas only once a month. From Chitutu, in the Songo country, we had to send to Silva Porto in Bié, a distance of over 200 miles. The mailman was generally away three weeks, traveling the 400 miles on foot and usually carrying a 60-pound load as well as the mail. With the mail, he often carried money, as the nearest place we could exchange checks for Portuguese currency was in Silva Porto. On one occasion the mailman left his load in a grass hut at the Luandu River, while he went to draw water to cook his evening meal. Some Africans were burning the long grass near by, and the hut caught fire. We lost a whole month's mail and a considerable sum of money as well.

While we were at Luma-Casai in Chokweland, an old African friend, called Samundengo, used to go for the mail to Moxico, and later to Vila Luso, after the railway was built. One week he went as usual and was on his way back with the mailbag. When he came to the Casai River, he was hungry and stopped at the river bank to light a fire and cook a meal. He then went down to the water's edge to wash his tin plate. He was squatting on his heels rinsing it, when there was a swirl in the water, a crocodile snapped, catching his two hands; he overbalanced and fell into the river. He was never seen again. He lost his life bringing the missionaries their mail.

A great problem was the fact that mail was often tampered with en route. When we were married, some friends of my wife in Providence, Rhode Island, had a wedding shower for her. The presents were packed up into thirteen parcels and sent by first class mail. At that time the post office would not insure parcels for Angola. Only one parcel eventually arrived and we never found out what happened to the other twelve. After several years, on our first furlough home from Angola, the friends in Providence told us of some of the contents of the lost parcels. Among other things was a complete set of curtains for the windows of our first little home in the Songo country. We asked the folks not to tell us any more; we felt too badly about it.

After this incident, I asked the post office to make an inquiry, to see if the stealing could be traced. When the inquiry reached the local post office in Silva Porto, I received an angry letter from the postmaster stating that I had accused them of stealing, and from that date, my mail would be handed only to me in person and would not be intrusted to any African mailman! Actually I had not accused anyone. As going in person would have entailed a walk of 400 miles every month, in desperation we had to arrange to have our mail sent by a different route via Malange, which was even further away than Silva Porto! But here too we had the same problem. Sometimes parcels were opened and baby shoes, etc., taken out. Sometimes the *National Geographic Magazine* would arrive minus the maps. We could not win.

Later on the trouble with stealing came to a head. For some years, after we moved back to Capango in Bié, we had an arrangement with a Portuguese trader, at the nearest point on the railway, to act as our agent in handling mail and in forwarding trunks and supplies which arrived by train from the coast. We had known this man for years, his daughters had been very kindly treated by the lady missionaries, and we regarded them all as warm personal friends. Over a period of several years, we had been losing things sent from home. When a missionary came back from overseas, the trunks had been opened somewhere en route, and about one third of the contents extracted. The same was happening with parcels sent through the post office. We hadn't a clue as to where it was happening.

But one day we had gone to the railway station to bid farewell to a missionary leaving for England, and the daughter of our Portuguese agent was standing on the platform of the station. My wife came over to me, trembling, and said: "That girl is wearing one of our daughter's dresses, which must have been taken out of one of our trunks when we came back from furlough!"

"Maybe you are mistaken," I replied. "It is a serious thing to accuse anyone of stealing, unless you are dead sure." The girl had hurriedly covered up the dress with an overcoat when she saw us. But it was the first indication we had as to what was happening. Later we had another clue, connected with a pair of pinking shears. Shears of this type were very rare in those days, and we had lost a pair, taken out of a trunk.

But the climax came a few months later, when we were again at the railway station to welcome a new couple from overseas. The same girl was on the station platform, and one of the lady missionaries came to me and said excitedly: "That girl is wearing my skirt!" I asked her to go back and take a good look and be absolutely sure she was making no mistake. When she assured me that she was certain, I decided to go to the authorities and ask their advice. The Portuguese administrator told me to approach the father and tell him what we had seen.

"If he acts nasty," said the administrator, "come back and tell me, and I will send the soldiers to search his house and store."

Some of the other missionaries came with me when I went to interview the agent. We felt very uncomfortable in approaching a man, whom we had regarded as a friend for many years, on such an errand. I told him what we had seen and of the episode of the pinking shears. He sent for his daughter and asked her to bring the shears. I was able to identify them as being taken out of our trunk. The father said: "If you think that this stealing has been happening in my home, you are welcome to search the place."

"That is what we have come for," I said. He called in a couple of Africans and had some large trunks brought in. The first one smelled of mothballs and was full of Portuguese and Madeira needlework. But the second one we opened was crammed full of clothing and bed linen taken out of our trunks and parcels. A young missionary couple had been married recently and we found some of their wedding presents, with the greeting cards still on them, among the loot. There were cutlery and dishes in the china cabinet in the kitchen.

The Portuguese trader stood silently by with an ashen face, while his daughter got down on her knees and confessed that she was the culprit. The father must have known what was going on, but the daughter accepted the blame. I asked her to show me how she had opened the trunks which had good locks and she had no key. She took me out to the store at the side of the house and showed me a hammer and chisel and a very fine nail punch. Instead of tampering with the locks, she had lifted the flanges covering the hinges at the back of the trunks, and then knocked out the pin holding the two sides of the hinge together with the fine punch. It was then easy to lift the lid from the back. After helping herself to what she wanted, the pin was replaced and the flange folded over the ends. We feel sure that she must have had the help or connivance of a man, as it was all so neatly done.

We refused to prosecute, although the administrator was anxious that we press charges. For the sake of our work, we felt it was better that it should not reach the law court. But we insisted that they return all that they had stolen and compensate us for what had been used. Some time later, an African turned up at our house at Capango with a huge sack tied with string and sealed with sealing wax. It was from the agent and his daughter. When we opened it, a pair of rubber boots tumbled out, along with a five-cell flashlight, a canteen of silver, as well as a host of other articles. These had been sent down country to a married daughter. Many other things we never recovered. Needless to say we changed our agent!

In 1941, during the war, our mail was held up by the Portuguese authorities in Lisbon for eleven months. Portuguese ships had been stopped by the Allied blockade, their mail too was being censored by the British authorities in Cape-town. In retaliation the Portuguese held up the mail of British and American citizens living in their colonies. After some protest through diplomatic channels, it was released. One evening we received it in a heap. There was not much sleep that night, as we sorted out and read a whole year's mail! When the war was over, we received some letters which had been captured by German forces when they occupied France. Mail from England came overland through France and Spain to Lisbon in Portugal, from whence it was shipped out to Angola by sea. Some of these letters contained money and checks, but although four years later, everything was intact.

When we moved to Capango in Bié, the mail came once a week, a welcome change from the once a month of earlier days. The mailman had to go 35 miles each way. For a time we had a young man who did the return trip in a day on foot. That meant that he traveled close to 70 miles a day. He started off very early in the morning, kept up a steady jog trot all day, and usually got back just after sunset. We tried to advise him to take two days to do the journey, as we were afraid he would damage his heart, but he preferred to do it that way.

A word of advice to those who write letters to missionaries: there is nothing more heart-warming and encouraging than to get news from home. The airmail service is a great boon and the inexpensive overseas air letter is the best bargain in the world. But please do not sermonize or engage in pious platitudes. The missionary is very human and he wants news from home. Tell him of the activities of his friends, of those who have been married or sick. Don't be afraid of a little bit of gossip of the right kind. News of meetings and Bible conferences, too, are always welcome. There is no need for a long epistle; a few cheery lines are a great tonic.

Indigenous Versus Mission-Supported Churches

Some years ago, while I was still at Chitutu, I had the opportunity of discussing methods of missionary work in Africa with two prominent men, leaders in their respective spheres.

The first, a doctor in charge of a mission hospital and at the same time field superintendent of his board, told me that the backbone of their work is the African evangelists and out-school teachers. These men have all been educated at the expense of the mission. Each was given a substantial subsidy to get married, his house and furniture were provided out of mission funds, and a salary was guaranteed, paid by Christians from abroad. Then came a financial depression and, as the money was not forthcoming, salaries had to be cut and in some cases stopped altogether. The work was threatened with utter collapse. The missionary bought a number of sets of carpentry and cobbling tools and offered them to the African workers, with the suggestion that they would be a help in earning their living while carrying on their work. In many cases the tools were contemptuously refused. One after another of the "evangelists" dropped out. Some went into commerce and actually became antagonistic to the mission. The missionary told me that this gave him a severe shock and led him to see that the mistake had been made at the beginning; that the foundation of the work was shaky. It was most difficult to make a change in a system which had been going on for fifty years.

The other missionary was in charge of one of the largest and most prosperous denominational missions in Angola. He had spent large sums of money, running into hundreds of thousands of dollars, on fine buildings, plant, and equipment. He confessed to me that he had made a huge mistake. If for any reason the foreigner has to leave the country, the African Christians are so poor that they would not be able to keep the buildings in repair and they would fall into ruin. He confessed to me, "You people who keep to simple buildings and simple methods are very much wiser."

In some quarters today there is a tendency to belittle "living by faith." In some places African workers are paid a salary for doing the Lord's work and the missionary excuses this by saying, "I cannot have faith for somebody else." To our mind he is denying his brother the privilege of complete dependence on God. The paid agent is asked by the heathen, "How much do you get for your work?" The impression is created that he is the servant of the white man. The principle, too, of handing out medicines, garments, food, etc., gratuitously is open to question. It breeds parasites, and brings people who believe for what they get out of it. But the main difficulty is in the fact that, if this principle is once started, it is almost impossible to change it, without threatening the very existence of the work. Thus the vital importance of incorporating indigenous principles in the foundation. Simple living by the missionary, the cultivation of the grace of giving in the national believers, and then looking and praying to God to raise up gifted nationals to step out in faith, seems to be the better plan.

It is generally agreed today that the objective of all missionary endeavor is the establishment of the indigenous church. It is certainly the teaching of the New Testament. From the practical standpoint of present-day trends, it is basic to the future of missions in every part of the world. Briefly described, it is the principle whereby missionaries, rather than acting as leaders themselves in the local areas where they have evangelized, look to God and the work of the Holy Spirit to raise up gift among the converts to take over leadership in the church, as well as initiative in evangelizing their own people. The three "selfs" — self-government, self-support, self-propagation — have been listed as the main factors in the indigenous principle. Under it, foreign funds are never used to support national teachers and evangelists, nor to erect their church buildings. The testimony for Christ, which by God's help the missionary has established, must take firm root, becoming native or indigenous to its new soil.

Therefore the function of the missionary is essentially that of a good parent: he stays with the children, helping, training, teaching them until they are mature adults. The good parent does not seek to make his children forever dependent on him for material support. The wise missionary likewise looks forward to the day when his spiritual children will be able to stand on their own feet and carry on the work, in dependence on God alone. Paul, the first missionary, carried on his great program in the provinces of the Roman Empire with the indigenous principle in mind, as a careful reading of the Acts and the Church Epistles will show. And he did it from the start.

We, too, had to learn these lessons the hard way, by a process of trial and error, by making mistakes and trying to correct them. But at least we could see the mistakes that the early pioneers had made and we tried to avoid them. The overrunning of China by communism, and what had happened to expensive missionary buildings and institutions in the land, was an example before our eyes and we sought to take the lesson to heart.

As the country opened up and dirt roads were cut through the forest, the automobile made travel much easier and expansion took place almost immediately. Some of the young men and women who had been raised in our school were keen Christians. They married and went out to new places to build their homes, taking the gospel with them. They were not supported financially by the mission but earned their living by agriculture. The Songo country was very suitable for cultivating rice and they concentrated on that. The Lord prospered them materially as well as spiritually. Each morning before they went to their work they sang a hymn, read the Scriptures, and prayed. Every night a meeting was held around a campfire. We visited them from time to time, treated them as fellow workers in the gospel, supplied them with literature and school materials.

They had their difficulties and were often persecuted by mean local officials. One young couple had worked hard to cut out new fields from virgin bush. They had planted manioc, which takes two or three years to mature, and from the flour of which they get their daily food. In the meantime they and their children had gone on short rations, waiting for the day when the fields would yield abundantly. Then a minor official decided, on a whim, to straighten out and widen the road. The new part of the road was cut right through the middle of the African couple's fields, and the work and hopes of several years were destroyed. There is no redress, compensation, or right of appeal to acts of this kind. Any protest would have met with blows and abuse.

In spite of everything the work spread, slowly and unpretentiously, but surely; first the daily meetings, then a school for the children, then changed regenerated lives, then baptism and the local church.

At the beginning we were so anxious to help at these outposts that we put up the first meeting room, furnished the doors and windows, the planks for seats, and a table. This was our first mistake. We never repeated it. The people regarded the building as belonging to the white man. Did he not build it and do a lot of the labor with his own hands? Anything that needed replacement or repair, it was his responsibility to do. The door could fall off its hinges and the roof cave in from the ravages of white ants, but the African never would think of lifting a hand to prevent it. It seemed to be a part of their mentality. Later we let them put up their own buildings and pay for them. Sometimes they were ramshackle affairs but at least they were their own.

We acted on the same principle in the schools and the dispensary. An African teacher taught in the school and had to be paid. We reminded the parents that it was their responsibility to pay the teacher. It was difficult at first, and they needed constant prodding to get them to pay up. Always at the back of our minds was the idea, some day these people will have to stand alone, and what then? They have to pay enormous fees to their witch doctors for phony concoctions that often poison them, and so why not pay for good medicine which can save their lives? No one was ever turned away because he could not pay. The genuine poor were always sympathetically helped. The problem was to maintain the delicate balance between undermining the people's self-respect by handouts, and obeying the scriptural command, "Freely ye have received, freely give."

After sixteen years' work among the Songo and Chokwe people at Chitutu, 11 outposts had been established, each with a group of believers and some with a primitive school. As soon as there was a nucleus of responsible elders, with an intelligent knowledge of the Scriptures, we encouraged them to establish the local church. They were autonomous from the start. We never presumed to dictate or talk down to them in a patronizing way. If they made mistakes, as they often did, we would suggest that there was a better way. There was mutual respect and affection between the African believers and their white brothers in Christ. As the work developed, it was suggested that a conference be held every three months, rotating around the various outposts. These were times of great joy and progress. The Africans were entirely responsible for the arrangements and for the entertainment of visitors. These gatherings gave opportunity for the teaching of the Word and also for the discussion of difficulties. While the young people would sing into the wee small hours, the elders often would spend a good part of the night huddled around a fire, threshing out the weighty problems of policy or procedure in the church, or maybe some complicated case of discipline. The missionary usually went to bed at a respectable hour and left them to it.

An outstanding feature of the work in Angola as a whole has been the planting and spontaneous growth of these local assemblies. They all conform to a pattern. It is a vivid illustration of the. parable of Mark 4:26-29: *"So is the kingdom of God, as if a man should cast seed into the ground, and should sleep, and rise night and day, and the seed should spring and grow up, he knoweth not how. For the earth bringeth forth fruit of herself; first the blade, then the ear,*

*after that the full corn in the ear. But when the fruit is brought forth,
immediately he putteth in the sickle, because the harvest is come."*

Perhaps the most remarkable story of the spontaneous spread
of the gospel in Angola is connected with a man called Silivondela, whom I knew well at Hualondo in Bié. He was married, had a
family, and was one of the elders in the church at Hualondo.

The work at Hualondo was pioneered and built up by
George Murrain, a well-educated and cultured colored missionary from Georgetown, British Guiana. Silivondela was
converted and taught under Mr. Murrain's preaching. I lived
at Hualondo and helped take care of the work when Mr. Murrain went to America in 1924-1925. Two years before I came to
Angola in 1924, a request came to Mr. Murrain from the local
government post for 28 men to carry loads to the coast. There
were circumstances which aroused suspicion as to the good
faith of the official who sent the order, and consequently there
was some difficulty in getting the full quota of men. Eventually
the 28 men, most of them professing Christians, were sent, and
assurances were received that they would return to their homes
when the work was done. The men left with their loads, but the
promises were not fulfilled, for the men disappeared. After sev-
en years, Silivondela returned to his home, where I happened to
be at the time, and told me the story of his experiences.

When he and the other men were drafted and had carried
their loads to the coast, they received no pay, but were hurried
on board a ship bound for a Portuguese island on the equator,
off the coast of Africa, called San Tome. It is a hot unhealthy
place and is covered with cocoa plantations called rotas. The
labor to work them was recruited by force from the mainland
in Angola. It was slavery in disguise. When the men arrived on
the island, they were separated from each other and distributed
among the plantation owners. The climate was much warmer
and more humid than the African highlands, from whence the
men had come; consequently the mortality was high. Silivondela said that, as he sat beside the fire at night after his long
hard day's work was done, he felt like weeping as he thought
of his wife and children and the friends he had left behind. The
possibility of ever seeing them again was very remote.

Silivondela was fortunate in having a hymnbook and portions of the Scriptures in his Umbundu language, and each night, sitting at the fire, he would sing and pray to keep up his spirits. Some of his fellow laborers were attracted by the words and melodies, and as he explained their meaning, some were convicted and led to faith in Christ through this fireside ministry. He asked his foreman for permission to hold meetings more publicly, but was told that all his time belonged to the company and that his request could not be granted. Two men were placed at the door of his hut with orders to tie him up if he did any more singing or praying. The foreman also forced him to do the heaviest sort of lifting.

"I did my best," he said, "without complaint, and I think that God gave me special strength, so that I did not break down."

In spite of opposition the movement grew and many became bold followers of Christ. Silivondela organized secret night schools, where the new converts were taught how to read and write. They had no books except the precious hymnbook and the Scriptures brought from Angola. Silivondela was able to earn some money through working overtime, and with this he bought paper and ink. At night he laboriously copied out the Scriptures and hymnbook by hand. These were used as textbooks in the school. As each new convert learned to read and write, he took up the work of copying, and the work rapidly increased.

Tobacco smoking and snuff-taking were discontinued to such an extent that the small traders, who sold these things, inquired and got to know the reason. Consequently fresh persecution broke out. Many of the converts suffered severely, but, as in similar cases in Church history, persecution only fanned the flames of revival. While these events were happening, similar scenes were transpiring in other parts of the island.

One day a number of native soldiers raided a village in Angola and carried off ten Christian men, among them Canangan-ja. This man, like the others, had heard the gospel and had been truly converted. On their way to San Tome, these ten men covenanted to be true to Christ at all costs and each of them racked his memory for all he could recall of passages of Scripture, which were then written down on any odds and ends of writing material on which they could lay their hands. They had been taken away from their homes suddenly and had no opportunity of returning, so not one of them had a book of any description. Later Cananganja prayed for a copy of the Scriptures, and his prayers were answered by discovering the Gospels of Matthew and Mark in Umbundu in the possession of another plantation hand, who, as he could not read, was quite willing to part with them. These, too, Cananganja copied out by candlelight into old diaries or exercise books, and these circulated among the plantation workers, of whom many more became Christians. One of these handwritten manuscripts of Scripture portions is now in the possession of the British and Foreign Bible Society in London.

A plantation foreman confiscated and burned a number of these precious books; but when he was preparing to burn a second batch, he could not get his matches to light, and he gave up the attempt, smitten by superstitious awe! Later Cananganja came to know Silivondela; they were of the same tribe and spoke the same language. In due course, Cananganja and two others of the original ten returned to Angola. Silivondela continued on with the work. He too was repatriated after seven years' work. I knew him well as an outstanding and gracious servant of God. He died of tuberculosis at his home at Hualondo in Bié.

Thus an entirely indigenous work developed, without the help of any missionary, until, scattered all over the island, there are large numbers of believers. At first they had to meet secretly, but on some of the plantations it was observed that becoming Christians usually made their laborers better workers, so gradually they were granted more liberty. Various missionaries have visited them from time to time. Eduardo Moreira, from Portugal, was able to take in some copies of the Scriptures in Umbundu. An Australian missionary couple, who had been working in Northern Brazil, on their way back to Australia, hearing of the need, spent the best part of a year on San Tome. They gained the affection and confidence of the people and were able to do a great deal of quiet work for Christ. Since then workers from Portugal have spent various periods on the island.

Another interesting example of the spontaneous operation

of the Holy Spirit has been a remarkable awakening and revival at Camashilu in north-central Angola. George Wise-man, from Buila in Chokweland, and Robert Allison, from Saurimo in the Lunda district, both experienced missionaries, have shepherded this work from the beginning. It was started by two Africans, Francisco and Muido. The latter is a Chokwe from Saurimo, taught by Mr. Allison. Francisco is a Lu-unda man who was sent on contract labor to the island of San Tome, where he heard the gospel and was converted through the work of the above-mentioned Africans. He is a John-the-Baptist type, completely fearless and a tireless evangelist. There is not a village or river-bank in the area where he hasn't preached. Robert Allison, in a letter dated August 1957 to the missionary magazine, *Echoes of Service*, described a visit to Camashilu with George Wiseman:

> "Mr. Wiseman and I have just returned from the Shinji country again and what we witnessed this time was something to be seen to be believed. We had heard some stories of a great spiritual upheaval going on among them. Even the Portuguese officials told us of it; traders commented on it; and it all sharpened our curiosity as we hastened towards them. Our faith was small indeed. At our first meeting in Camashilu proper there were approximately 500 listening to the gospel and we were amazed at the good number and interest.
>
> "'But,' said the believers, 'the people have not come yet.' In the morning at 6:00 o'clock, 1,000 were there waiting for us to get out of our camp beds for the gospel meeting. All that day they kept streaming in to the encampment—men, women, and children. It was a sight to see the menfolk, almost every one armed with a loaded gun. When they stood and spoke to you, you were looking right down the barrel, and one was not too comfortable. These old guns have a nasty habit of going off at the wrong time! When we swung around to get a more comfortable side look at the gun, the owner invariably kept following us around in the circuit. But they stacked their guns before they sat around for the gospel story.

"That evening there were 2,000 people, and the following morning at 6:00 o'clock, when we went down to the river for some to be baptized, the place seemed black with people, fully 2,000 strong. One would have expected noise and disturbance but they stood around in a reverent manner as the message was given, and hushed as Mr. Wiseman entered the water to baptize. We had never dreamed that we would ever witness scenes like these.

"It was the awakening of an entire tribe. It was God doing something in a big way. This had nothing to do with us. It all happened during our absence, for the believers declared to us that this had been going on for some time. How we rejoiced before God that it was not the personality of the missionaries that was drawing them! The traders were complaining that they were not selling as much beer now to the Shinjis and also that the sale of images had fallen. Some of the believers were taken aside and asked what the missionaries were giving to them to get so many to come to the meetings. Answer—'A living Christ.'

"We had the honor of baptizing another 40 during this last trip and throughout the tribe there are now some sixteen places where regular gospel work is being carried on. Some believers walk as far as 25 miles at the weekend for the sake of breaking bread."

The work at Camashilu continues. The missionaries at Luma-Casai in Chokweland visit the area from time to time and help with its development and consolidation.

Back to Bié

After sixteen years' pioneer work among the Chokwe and Songo people at Chitutu, we were forced to come to some heart-rending decisions. We came to the conclusion that the time had come to move our base back to Bié, about 200 miles to the west. This was the area in which I had worked when first coming to the country in 1924. There were various reasons for this move. During our years at Chitutu, the work had spread, but principally in one direction—among the Songo people towards the west. In the north and east, the Chokwe population had gradually declined until the country was almost depopulated. There was increasing unrest among the people, owing to oppressive conditions.

At first the people had to pay a rather small hut tax. Every man between the ages of sixteen and sixty had to pay it. Then the tax was suddenly doubled. After a couple of years it was raised again. It became impossible for the people to find the money to pay the tax. A man who hid in the bush and paid no tax was called a *chombo* ("wild pig"). If found, he was flogged. Those who did not pay within an allotted time were sent away on contract labor for eighteen months, either to the diamond mines or to the sugar plantations or railway construction at the coast. The eighteen months' work paid two years' tax and a little left over to bring home. They usually arrived home with the equivalent of about five dollars.

As well as this system of contract labor, the people had to work for long periods on the roads without pay. They had to provide their own tools and food. Men, women, and even children were forced to do this work. Quotas of men and women had to work at the local government post and in the cleaning and harvesting at wild coffee plantations belonging to the authorities. All this, too, was unpaid forced labor. Native soldiers, called *cipaios*, roamed the countryside with a hippo-hide whip, carrying out these orders. They were merciless on their own people.

The Chokwes, who are a proud and spirited people, could not take it. They started burning their villages and running away in the middle of the night. Reports had come in of wonderful conditions in the Dilolo area of the Congo and of a land of promise in Northern Rhodesia (now Zambia), where lots of money could be made at the copper mines. Some of these stories were exaggerated, but there was enough truth in them to cause discontent. Night after night, old friends came to our door under cover of darkness to bid us good-bye. We hated to see them go, but under the circumstances could not blame them.

Inside of a year there were few Chokwes left in the area. Today there are more than 100,000 Chokwes in the Congo and in Zambia. In southwestern Katanga they have spread as far as Kasaji. Their language is the predominant one in the district. Many of them are Christians and in church fellowship.

The Songos are a more docile people than the Chokwes. They are loyal to their chiefs and to their country. They did not run away, but their numbers were seriously depleted by this wholesale labor exploitation.

On a number of occasions I tried to approach the Portuguese authorities in a diplomatic way about what was happening. Young people were being taken away from our schools for contract labor to such an extent that it became almost impossible to carry on. Several times I protested to the officials responsible and was told that this was the only way that the demands of the labor market at the coast could be met. Soon matters came to a head.

A young Songo man, a Christian, was captured by native soldiers, and sent to the diamond mines for eighteen months, in the usual way. When he returned, he went back to his regular occupation of fishing. One day, a wooden rack on which he was standing, where he was spreading out his day's catch to dry in the sun, collapsed. As he fell, a fishing spear, standing point up, entered his body between his legs. He was seriously ill for a time, but recovered. As soon as he was able to walk, some soldiers came around, tied him up, and took him to the fort to be sent away again as a contract laborer. He al-ready had the money to pay his tax, so there was no excuse on that grounds. He also was the sole support of his old mother.

I decided to make him a test case. I wrote a letter in the most respectful and mildest of terms to the Portuguese administrator, explaining the circumstances and begging his intervention in the case. I received a very sharp reply warning me that if I, who was a foreigner and a missionary, ever interfered again in government affairs, I would be asked to leave the country! I could see that I was up against an impossible situation.

The decision to move our base back to Bié was not easy to make. We loved the Songo people, had seen considerable blessing among them, and had done some translation work of the Scriptures into their language. But the serious depletion of the population forced us to the conclusion that it would be wise to make our headquarters among the Ovimbundu people to the west, and visit the Songo people periodically. In 1940 we moved to Capango in Bié.

It was an interesting experiment to leave a comparatively new work without a missionary for a number of years. It tested the caliber of the Songo believers. They responded magnificently. New places were opened for the gospel. At the end of ten years the work had doubled. Sometimes elders from Bié came out to help with ministry, but usually they were dependent on local preachers. The Songo brethren, who carried the burden of the work, earned their living by growing rice. They hired teachers to carry on elementary schools to teach the children. Some of the more intelligent boys were sent to the boarding school at Capango in Bié. When they came back, they helped in teaching in their own villages.

Then the government stepped in. They sent us an ultimatum

that unless a full-time missionary were to go back to Chitutu in the Songo tribe, they would close down the work. As no one else was available at that time to go, we went back for a year, re-erected the buildings, and reorganized the school and medical work. Then a young missionary couple, Mr. and Mrs. Jack King, who had been working at Capango in Bié, offered to go and take over the work. They quickly learned the Songo language, continued the translation work, and in spite of many difficulties, saw considerable development and blessing. A flourishing work among lepers was started and many of these afflicted people became Christians. At the beginning of 1961 there were twenty-two places in the Songo tribe where the gospel had taken root, each with a company of believers operating on an indigenous basis, spreading the evangel among their own people.

The last twenty years of our service in Angola were spent at Capango in Bié. This is an old established work, the beginnings of which are described earlier in this book. Numerically, the greatest success in missionary work in Angola has taken place among the Umbundu-speaking people in this area. The United Church of Canada, the American Board of Commissioners for Foreign Missions, and the Philafricaine Mission from Switzerland also work among the Ovimbundu.

As far as the assemblies of Brethren are concerned, it is our oldest work in Angola, and has been going on continuously for seventy-five years. There are many third-generation Christians. It is quite common to meet men and women who have been believers for over fifty years.

Up until 1930, when it was still possible to have general conferences, 3,000 people would gather together for three or four days for the ministry of the Word. When these became too unwieldy, regional conferences were held at the various centers, those at Chilonda and Capango often attracting between 1,000 and 2,000 people. All the arrangements for feeding the people, for ministry, and for finances were, and still are, in the hands of African brethren. There is no domination or competition between the white missionary and his African brothers, but mutual respect and courtesy. African preachers are responsible for most of the Bible teaching and preaching at these conferences. Altogether there must be about 250 companies of African believers in Bié speaking the Umbundu language. Many of these are fully organized autonomous assemblies, while others just have gospel meetings and work among young people. This, of course, does not include the large work being done by the above-mentioned denominational bodies in adjacent areas.

The greatest part of this work has been done by African young men who have gone to new places, built houses, cut out fields, and earn their living either by a trade or by agriculture. At the same time they carry on meetings, preach the gospel, and teach the Word. All of them are self-supporting. In the case of a school teacher, and most villages where there are Christians there is a school, he is supported by the parents of the pupils. In this way the message of the gospel has been propagated along natural lines. Among these groups of African believers there are many weaknesses and much failure, but it is very evident that the Holy Spirit has been at work. It has been proven once again that wherever apostolic New Testament principles are put into practice, they will have apostolic results.

When we first returned to Capango in 1940 there were only two single ladies on the station, Annie Gammon and Grace Smith. Two years later Grace died after twenty-three years of faithful service for the Lord there. Shortly after our coming, Walter Gammon arrived from England and served at Capango until May 1967. In 1951 Mr. and Mrs. Alan Adcock came also from England. Both Walter and Alan were born of missionary parents in Africa.

Annie Gammon, Walter's aunt, had been at Capango since the commencement of the work in 1905. The last twenty-three years of her life she spent continuously in Africa and refused to go overseas on furlough. She made it a habit of life to rise at 4:00 a.m. for a time of devotion with the Lord and her Bible. Most of her later years were spent in great pain but she never complained. She was a saintly soul and an inspiration to us all. She was affectionately known to the missionaries as "Auntie Nin." She served the Lord for fifty-three years at Capango, dying when she was eighty-seven years old, and is buried in the little graveyard on the edge of the African forest. There four other missionaries, who have given their lives for Christ in His service, also lie.

My chief interest at Capango was running regional Bible schools, not only in the immediate area in Bié, but much further afield. Again the object was to train and equip the African elders for the day when they might be without the help of the white missionary. On the one hand we were anxious to avoid creating a clerical class, a cut higher than their fellows, but on the other hand we realized the great need for sane, spiritual leaders who could intelligently shepherd the flock.

The Africans, being mostly small farmers and self-employed, had slack periods in the year, between sowing and harvest, when they were free to come together for two or three weeks. I arranged to be with them at this time. The school usually had three daily sessions of two hours each—morning, afternoon, and evening. With fellow workers in the area we set out a systematic course of study to be followed.

It usually conformed to the following pattern:

A New Testament book study, such as Romans or First Corinthians.

A character study, including the lives of Abraham, Joseph, David, Peter, Paul, John, etc.

Doctrine: redemption, justification, sanctification, and related themes.

Church truth: its universal and local aspects, the ordinances, worship, church government.

The Person of Christ: His deity, humanity, death, resurrection, priesthood, and coming again.

There was no rigid rule about following a curriculum, but, depending on local circumstances and the need for emphasis in any particular situation, we tried to teach and build up the Christians in the great truths of the faith.

Each session lasted an hour, with a brief rest period at the interval. All the teaching was in the African vernacular and opportunity was given for questions and answers and discussion. The men were given typewritten notes, copied on a duplicator, of all the studies, which they could carry home and read at their leisure. These notes had to be written both in the vernacular and in the Portuguese language to conform to the law.

The feeding of the men was not a problem as the schools were held in their local villages. They lived at home and the school sessions were held in the local meeting room. Simplicity was the watchword. All the equipment required was a blackboard, some chalk, and the typewritten notes. It was a joy to see the growth in spiritual things of some of the men, and to hear that the studies were being reproduced and developed in their ministry among their own people. It was quite a common thing to see as many as 200 men from strategic parts of the country coming to these study sessions and expressing their appreciation for help received.

For many years I made a practice of spending Sunday with a company of African believers in the villages, sharing in their worship and gospel meetings. At first I took a lunch with me, but decided that this was raising a barrier and gave them the idea that I would not eat their food. When I left the lunch box behind, they were delighted to entertain me with the best they had. Sometimes it was boiled rice and fried eggs, at other times manioc mush and a cooked chicken. They never offered me the stewed caterpillars or the toasted locusts which they ate themselves. Their manners and etiquette were above reproach as they sought to entertain their white guest. But the ultimate came when they started to offer me money to pay for the gasoline to run the car which had brought me to them. My first reaction was to refuse it, as I did not want to give the impression that I wanted compensation for coming. But it would have been an insult not to take it. I accepted it as from the Lord and thanked God that they had a heart like the Macedonians who, in the abundance of their joy and their deep poverty, abounded unto the riches of their liberality.

In the light of changes in other parts of Africa, we pray that the day may never come when these delightful relationships between the simple African believers and the men who brought them the gospel will ever be altered.

Epilogue

The foreign missionary is a guest in the land where he works. He does not interfere in its politics. He respects and obeys its laws. His sphere is in spiritual matters; he leaves the making of laws, and their application to the daily life of the people, to the civil administration. It must be remembered that, when Paul wrote to the Roman Christians: *"Let every soul be subject to the higher powers. For there is no power but of God: the powers that be are ordained of God,"* a wicked despot was on the throne, and that later Paul was to lose his life at his hands. Missionaries have consistently taught the African believers their duty to the state, to obey its laws, and to be good citizens. There may have been exceptions, where certain missionaries with radical ideas have stepped out of their sphere, but this has been the general rule.

After seventy years of missionary work in Angola, between the two world wars a new world-wide movement was born. Countries that had been under the yoke of the invader for centuries, began to awake from sleep. Zealous national patriots arose who demanded freedom and independence. Colonialism became a bad word. Southern Ireland, Egypt, India, Burma, and Syria, one after another became independent states.

Then the nationalistic movement hit Africa. The sleeping giant started to come to life. In 1960 no less than seventeen new

African nations became independent members of the United Nations. With some, like Tanzania and Zambia, the change from European colonial rule to self-government was a peaceful and bloodless transition, but in the Congo it was different. Under Belgian administration the country was progressing slowly but surely, but when the Belgians hurriedly left in 1960 it went back to primitive savagery and chaos. These events had repercussions in neighboring Angola.

Pressure is being brought to bear on the Portuguese to get out and hand over the country to the Africans. Let it be said at once that there is no comparison between the Belgian and the Portuguese administrations. The two systems were very different. The Portuguese claim that Angola is not a colony but is an overseas province of Portugal. They have been in Angola since 1482, a period of nearly 500 years, and have no intention of ever handing it over to the Africans.

Up until 1960 there was no visible evidence of any revolutionary movement inside Angola. But the happenings in the neighboring Congo and other African countries have had a tremendous impact. A movement was organized in Kinshasa, formerly Leopoldville, in the Congo by Africans who had fled from Angola, and is headed by a man called Holden Roberto. It is called U.P.A. (Union of the Populations of Angola). A rival movement is known as P.M.L.A. (Popular Movement for the Liberation of Angola). Both movements want independence for the African in Angola. They have organized camps in the Congo for the arming and training of guerrillas against the Portuguese.

The tragic events which took place in Angola in February 1961 focused attention on the country. The first action took place in the capital city of Luanda on February 4. A crowd of Angola Africans stormed the Sao Paulo jail and the police post. The attack was not successful and seven of the attackers were killed. The attack was renewed on February 5. This time the fighting and casualties were more extensive. The Portuguese police and troops had now gathered in force and were further strengthened by armed civilians. Then there began an indiscriminate slaughter of Africans. Nobody knows exactly how many were killed. Trucks came around and picked up the bodies, which were then taken out to a mass burial in the bush. At this time, my wife and I were coming home to the United States from Angola on board a Belgian freighter in the harbor at Luanda. We stayed for ten days while the ship was loading coffee. I went up to the town and had a meeting with the Africans. They gave me details and statistics of the massacre which I will not quote.

On March 15 there were reprisals. Groups of sullen Africans, natives of Angola, smarting under grievances and hiding in the forests of northern Angola and Cabinda, in what is now known as "the rotten triangle," on account of the murders which took place there, suddenly launched a campaign of terror and revenge. They invaded the homes of the Portuguese planters and officials, killing and mutilating about 200 men, women, and children.

From that time on, there has been much bloodshed and the end is not yet. The Portuguese have brought out to Angola a large army with modern weapons of war. Protestant missions and missionaries in the north of Angola have been made the scapegoat for the political troubles in the country. Thousands of innocent people have lost their lives. By July 1961, the American Methodists working in the Luanda and Malange areas reported the death of seventeen pastors at Portuguese hands. Thirty others were in prison, and a further ninety were missing. The Baptists in the north also suffered severely. In mid-June the British Baptist Missionary Society gave a careful estimate, admittedly approximate and yet based on a detailed survey, of evidence from many sides. They estimated that the Portuguese had killed some 20,000 African men, women, and children during the three months since the northern rising had begun. A Portuguese military officer told a newspaper correspondent in Luanda, some seven weeks after the rising, "I estimate that we've killed 30,000 of these 'animals.'" Many thousands have been tortured and killed since that time.

Some of the Africans mentioned in this book, whom I have known intimately for more than thirty years, have been executed. Early in 1961 I went around the various outposts in the Songo area, having meetings with the African believers, many of whom were our children in the faith. I tried to encourage and strengthen their hands in God. I little realized what lay ahead in the very near future.

A disgruntled native teacher, who had been dismissed for misconduct and who was thirsting for revenge, went to the authorities and charged the Christians with having nationalistic leanings. Eight of the leaders were arrested by the military and taken to the local administration. There they were beaten and tortured in order to extract a confession. Details are too horrible to describe. When the confession was not obtained, they were lined up on the edge of a pit and shot through the back of the neck.

One of the younger men, whom we have known since he was born, while the others were being executed, started to sing a hymn in his soft Songo language:

> Be not dismayed whate'er betide,
> God will take care of you,
> Under His sheltering wings abide,
> God will take care of you.

The officer was so surprised that he picked him out of the line and sent him back home, telling him to tell his friends what had happened to the others. This was done to frighten them.

The young African who was left in charge of what was formerly our home, was also taken to the local post and cross-questioned. When he denied the charges of disloyalty to the government, he was beaten with clubs, in the presence of the officer, by two traders, and left broken and dead at their feet. Many others were put in prison and others sent away on forced labor to distant places. The rank and file of the African believers had their Bibles taken from them and in some cases a Roman Catholic teacher installed in the meeting room where the believers met. A veteran Portuguese trader who knew all the men just mentioned, who were killed, has testified that there was no evidence against any of them. We, too, can testify that they were humble, hard-working, sincere souls who never were engaged in subversive activity of any kind.

There are still many places in Angola where the work goes on, in some cases under difficulties. Up until 1965 the Chokwe and Luena-speaking areas in the eastern part of the country were comparatively quiet and the work uninterrupted, but in 1966 guerrilla fighters, from across the border in Katanga and Zambia, started operations. Scattered over the area are many Christian communities and outposts. The guerrillas often come to these places at night, demanding food, shelter, and help. If this is refused, they burn the place down and kill the inhabitants. If it is given and the Portuguese authorities hear about it, they are liable to be arrested, imprisoned, and often executed. Thus the Christians find themselves between two fires.

Another disturbing feature is the fact that if a Protestant evangelical missionary has to leave the country for furlough, his visa to return is generally refused. Some missionaries, who were born in the country of missionary parents, and who have lived there all their lives, have been treated in this way. It looks as if evangelical missionaries are gradually being forced out of the country. We had to leave Angola in 1961 for health reasons. In 1962 I visited Portugal and, while there, made three requests for a visa to go back to Angola. All three requests were refused without explanation.

We are quite sure that God's gracious purposes for the out-calling of His Church will be completed and that whatever is genuine and solid will remain, although it be tried by fire. But the work of God in Angola today needs the fervent prayers and intercessions of God's people everywhere.

Bibliography

Arnot, Frederick S. Garenganze; Seven Years' Pioneer Mission Work in Central Africa. London: James E. Hawkins, 1889.

Arnot, F. S. Missionary Travels in Central Africa. London: Pickering & Inglis, 1914.

Baker, Ernest. Life and Explorations of Frederick Stanley Arnot. New York: Dutton, 1920.

Barns, T. Alexander. Angola Sketches. London: Methuen, 1928.

Blaikie, William G. Personal Life of Livingstone. London: John Murray, 1882.

Campbell, Dugald. In the Heart of Bantuland. Philadelphia: Lippincott, 1922.

A Central African Jubilee, 1881-1931. London: Pickering & Inglis, 1931. (Addresses at jubilee, and historical notes of various missions)

Childs, Gladwyn Murray. Umbundu Kinship and Character. London, New York, Toronto: Oxford, 1949.

Crawford, D. Thinking Black. London: Morgan & Scott, 1914.

Cushman, Mary Floyd. Missionary Doctor. New York: Harper, 1944.

De Lemos, Alberto. Historia de Angola. Lisbon: 1932.

Duffy, James. Portuguese Africa. Harvard, 1959.

Fisher, W. Singleton and Hoyte, Julyan. <u>Africa Looks Ahead</u>. London: Pickering & Inglis, 1948.

Gunther, John. <u>Inside Africa</u>. London: Hamish Hamilton, 1955.

Harris, John H. <u>Africa—Slave or Free</u>. London: Student Christian Movement, 1919.

Hambly, Wilfred Dyson. <u>Jamba</u>. Chicago: Pellegrini & Cudahy, 1947.

Historical Section of the Foreign Office. <u>Angola, Including Cabinda</u>. No. 120. London: His Majesty's Stationery Office, 1920.

Ingleby, Arthur G. <u>Pioneer Days in Darkest Africa</u>. London: Pickering & Inglis. (Biography of Charles A. Swan.)

Lawman, Tony. <u>From the Hands of the Wicked</u>. London: Robert Hale, 1960. (Biography of Frederick Stanley Arnot.)

Livingstone, David. <u>Livingstone's Travels and Researches in South Africa</u>. New York: Harper, 1858.

Moreira, Edwardo. <u>The Significance of Portugal</u>. London, New York, Toronto: World Dominion Press, 1933.

Nevinson, Henry W. <u>Fire of Life</u>. London: Nisbet, 1935.

Smith, Edwin W. <u>The Shrine of a People's Soul</u>. London: Edinburgh House, 1929.

Swan, Charles A. <u>The Slavery of Today</u>. Glasgow: Pickering & Inglis, 1909.

Tilsley, G. E. <u>Dan Crawford of Central Africa</u>. London: Oliphants, 1929.

Tucker, John T. <u>Angola: The Land of the Blacksmith Prince</u>. London, New York, Toronto: World Dominion Press, 1933.

Tucker, John T. <u>Drums in the Darkness</u>. Toronto: Ryerson, 1927.

Varian, H. F. <u>Some African Milestones</u>. Wheatley: Oxford, Ronald, 1953. (Building of Benguela Railway.)

Williams, Sir Ralph. <u>How I Became Governor</u>.

Wengatz, John C. <u>Miracles in Black</u>. New York: Revell, 1938.

On the Emergency of 1961:

Addicott, Len. Cry Angola. London: S.C.M., 1962.

Institute of Race Relations. Angola; A Symposium: Views of a Revolt. . London: Oxford, 1962.

Maciel, Artur. Angola Heroica. Lisbon: Livraria Bertrand, 1963.

Nielsen, Waldemar A. African Battleline: American Policy Choices in Southern Africa. New York: Harper & Row, 1965.

Okuma, Thomas. Angola in Ferment. Boston: Beacon, 1962.

On the Morning of March 15. Portuguese-American Committee on Foreign Affairs. Boston: 1961.

Report of the United Nations Sub-Committee on the Situation in Angola. General Assembly. Official Records, Sixteenth Session. Supplement No. 16 (A/4978). New York: 1962.

Zeiger, Henry A. The Seizing of the Santa Maria. New York: Popular Library, 1961.

Index